YESHUA
the
MESSIAH

by
DAVID CHERNOFF

Cover design by Steffi Rubin

YESHUA THE MESSIAH

COPYRIGHT © 1983 BY DAVID CHERNOFF

Fourth printing 1989

MMI Publishing Co.
P.O. Box 1024
Havertown, Pa. 19083
215-477-2706
Printed in the United States of America

CONTENTS

Introduction

Messianic Judaism, Messianic Jews, Jewish believers in Yeshua (Jesus in Hebrew).

Since 1967, we have seen Messianic Judaism grow before our very eyes. Today, this movement easily numbers in the tens of thousands in the United States alone.

Messianic synagogues have sprung up in nearly every major city in America, along with growing Messianic communities and day schools. In addition, we have seen the rise of Messianic music, books, records, television programs and huge Messianic conferences.

Obviously, this movement has stirred great controversy among both Jews and Christians. Some say that it is impossible to believe in Yeshua (Jesus) and still be Jewish, while others hail this movement as a fulfillment of biblical prophecy.

As one who has been involved in the Messianic movement for many years, I have felt the need for some time to write on the real key to this whole issue . . . Yeshua Himself!

Oftentimes, the person of Yeshua becomes lost in the shuffle of culture, history, religion and time. In fact, one of the greatest obstacles that faces Messianic Judaism is that during the past nineteen-hundred years, Yeshua has been completely uprooted from His Jewish background and heritage.

To believe in Yeshua has become a non-Jewish, or Gentile, religion.

This is particularly ironic in light of the fact that Yeshua was Jewish, as were His disciples, all the writers of the New Covenant

(Testament), the apostles and all of Yeshua's initial followers!!!

It is high time to get back to Yeshua's Jewish roots!

The goal of this book, therefore, is threefold.

First of all, it is to enumerate and clarify the misconceptions which cloud the Jewish Jesus, while at the same time placing Yeshua back within His authentic Jewish context.

Second, it is to show scripturally that Yeshua is truly the Jewish Messiah and Savior of Israel. While I did not go through every single Messianic prophecy, discussing them in-depth (for there is neither the time nor the space for that here), I chose instead to go through some of the major prophecies answering many of the questions critical to the Messiahship of this controversial figure from Galilee.

Finally, I wanted to show that historically and biblically it is Jewish to believe in Yeshua (Jesus).

Messianic Judaism did not begin in 1967 but rather in the first century A.D., when hundreds of thousands of Jewish people accepted Yeshua as their Messiah. Those early Messianic Jews did not feel that they had "converted" to another religion. On the contrary, they felt that they were "completed Jews" for having found the Jewish Messiah!

Today, Messianic Jews feel exactly the same way!

It is important for all of us to know whether or not Yeshua is truly the Messiah. If Yeshua did come to atone for our sins as the Suffering Messiah, then our very eternity is at stake.

With world events rushing toward their prophetic conclusion, with the threat of nuclear annihilation hanging over our heads and with the shadow of the great Russian Bear looming over the horizon, now is the time to make sure that we are right with our Creator.

Hopefully, this book will help you in drawing closer to God, and in making that all-important decision about the Messiahship of Yeshua.

David Chernoff

1

The Coming of the Messiah

For centuries, the ancient Jewish prophets foretold of One who was to come who would bring salvation and deliverance to God's Chosen People, Israel.

In their extensive writings that spanned nearly two millenia, they gave clear prophetic "signposts" by which Israel could recognize the "Anointed One" and be prepared to receive Him when He came.

HIS BIRTH

The Scriptures say His Name would be called Wonderful, Counsellor, the Mighty God, the Everlasting Father, the Prince of Peace, Root of Jesse, Holy One of Israel, Star out of Jacob, Immanuel ("God is with Us"), Shiloh ("He Whose Right it is"), Son of God, yet Son of Man.

He was to be born (Isaiah 9:5–6), supernaturally of a virgin (Isaiah 7:14), from the tribe of Judah (Genesis 49:10), of the royal seed of David (Isaiah 11:1–2).

He would not be born in the capital city of Jerusalem as so many might have expected, but in an inauspicious little town six miles to the south called Bethlehem. From this little town had come Israel's mightiest ruler, King David, and from this little town would come an even greater Ruler *whose goings forth are from long ago, from the days of eternity"* (Micah 5:1–2).

The Hebrew prophets were also not vague as to *when* the Messiah should appear upon the earth, in *Eretz Yisrael*, the land of Israel.

The great Jewish prophet, Daniel, said that the Messiah

would come before the destruction of the second temple, which occurred in 70 A.D. It was then that the Roman armies under Titus broke through the walls of Jerusalem, destroyed the temple, and razed the city to the ground.

HIS DEATH

Strangely enough, when the Messiah would come, the prophets said that He would not come as a great, conquering King but in meekness and humility. He would not enter Jerusalem as a great Warrior with victorious armies behind Him, but in humility on the back of a donkey (Zechariah 9:9–10).

While He would be a prophet in the mold of Moses (Deuteronomy 18:15–18) like so many of the prophets before Him, the Messiah would not be accepted by His people . . . at least not this time.

Instead, He would be despised and rejected of men (Isaiah 53:3). Mocked, beaten and spit upon (Isaiah 50:6, Psalm 22:7–8), He would finally be sold to His executioners for a paltry 30 pieces of silver . . . about $15 in today's currency (Zechariah 11:12).

He would be killed, like so many of the Jewish prophets before Him. He would not die by stoning but by the Roman method of execution, "crucifixion." King David, who was also a prophet, perfectly described how the Messiah's hands and feet would be pierced in crucifixion, centuries before the Romans ever became a world power (Psalm 22:16)!

In His death He would be executed with criminals (Isaiah 53:12) yet buried among the rich (Isaiah 53:9). Even His clothes would be distributed among His executioners by lot, so great would be His shame (Psalm 22:18).

HIS RESURRECTION

Yet, His death would not be a tragedy but it would become instead the greatest victory the universe had ever seen!

For God took the responsibility of the Messiah's death. *He* claimed to be the One to kill Him, and God said that it pleased Him to do it!

Why? Because He made the Messiah's soul an offering for our sins! He was to be our "Passover Lamb" without spot or blemish. He was to be our "Yom Kippur Scapegoat" (Day of Atonement), dismissing and carrying away our sins upon His back for eternity.

When this extraordinary offering was completed, God made it clear that He would not leave His Holy One in the grave, but would raise Him up in power and glory, conquering sin and death forever (Isaiah 53:10, Psalm 16:10).

Then the Messiah would ascend back into heaven to sit at the right hand of God (Psalm 110) to await His return to this earth.

HIS RETURN

For the Messiah *is* to come again, at the End of Days, when prophecy is near completion, and when all the nations of the earth have gathered against Israel (Zechariah 12:10).

Then He will descend with a shout, coming with victory and power to destroy the enemies of Israel, judging all the nations, punishing wickedness and rewarding righteousness (Zechariah 12:8-9).

Then all of Israel will know God, from the least of them to the greatest of them. And God said, ". . . and their sin I will remember no more" (Jeremiah 31:31-34).

At the same time, the Messiah will also become a "light to the nations, to open blind eyes, to bring out prisoners from the dungeon, and those who dwell in darkness from the prison" (Isaiah 42:6-7).

"Then the eyes of the blind will be opened, and the ears of the deaf will be unstopped. Then the lame will leap like a deer, and the tongue of the dumb will shout for joy. For water will break forth in the wilderness and streams in the Arabah. And the scorched land will become a pool, and the thirsty ground springs of water . . ." (Isaiah 35:5-7).

"And the wolf will dwell with the lamb, and the leopard will lie down with the kid, and the calf and the young lion and the fatling together; and a little boy will lead them" (Isaiah 11:6).

2

Predicting the Future

Throughout the Tenach (Old Testament), there are numerous prophecies about the Messiah.

All of these Messianic passages are but pieces to a gigantic, centuries-long jigsaw puzzle.

These Jewish prophets were supernaturally inspired by God to give revelation to man about this great Deliverer. He gave each of these men a glimpse of this Holy One, along with certain information to impart to the world about Him.

God's purpose was that we should study these passages to know about the Messiah. If we study and put this biblical puzzle together, we *can know* who the Messiah of Israel is.

Nor are these predictions in the Bible vague and therefore open to anybody's interpretation. These ancient seers were very specific when they wrote about Israel's coming Deliverer. They wanted to make sure that there was no mistaking such an important Personage when He came!

GOD'S SIGNATURE ON THE BIBLE

Imagine having your entire life from birth to death described by men years before you were even born!

''Centuries before the Messiah was born, His birth and career, His sufferings and glory, were all described in outline and detail in the Bible. The Messiah is the only Person ever born into the world whose ancestry, birthplace . . . manhood, teaching, character, career, preaching, reception, rejection, death, burial, resurrection and ascension were all prewritten in the most marvelous manner centuries before He was born.''[1]

Imagine, if you will, 20–25 Jewish prophets whose lives spanned some 1500 years, all perfectly describing the same man, the same Messiah of Israel!

One can only come to the conclusion that these predictions or prophecies are God's "Signature" on the Bible, and dramatic proof that the Bible is the living Word of God. Surely no man is capable of peering into the future with such accuracy.

HISTORY FORETOLD

These men predicted of nations and empires that would arise hundreds of years before they actually became world powers. They foretold of specific events, including Israel's 70 year captivity in Babylon, and the even greater worldwide dispersion of Israel that came in the 1st-century A.D.

The Tenach (Old Testament) even contains predictions that have come to pass in this century!

The prophets not only foretold of Israel's scattering to the four corners of the earth, but also of their regathering back into the land at the "End of Days." They spoke of the land blossoming under Israel's gentle care and of the nation being reborn in a single day.

Even more startling, though, are those numerous prophetic passages which are still unfulfilled, but which will all be fulfilled in our lifetimes: predictions about Russia, the Middle East, China, the AntiMessiah, empires to come, and of course the return of the Messiah Himself.

Someone truly described biblical prophecy as "history foretold."

"[Prophecy] demonstrates that the God of the Bible is both all-knowing to be able to foretell the future entwined around numberless men who are free moral agents, and all-powerful, to be able to bring to pass a perfect fulfillment of His Word in the midst of widespread unbelief, ignorance and rebellion on the part of men."[2]

God wants us to know what His Word says and who His Messiah is. There is only one real way to find that out, and that is to study the Tenach, the living Word of God.

As we put all the pieces of the jigsaw puzzle together, the picture comes sharply into focus. All the prophecies ultimately point to the only man in history who could have possibly fulfilled *every single prediction*, and that is Yeshua (Jesus in Hebrew) of Nazareth.

3

The De-Judaizing of Jesus

Never has such a figure dominated and influenced the course of human history so completely!

Over one billion people in the world today profess to be followers of this "Yeshua" (Jesus). Faith in this man of Galilee has spread geographically to almost every corner of the globe.

He is undoubtedly the most outstanding personage in history and yet so little is really understood about Him. Despite volumes upon volumes which have been written about Him, today there still exists a great deal of misconception and confusion about who Yeshua really was and is.

During the 2000 years since Yeshua walked the face of the earth, our perception of Him has undergone a dramatic and radical transformation. Notice that I did not say that Yeshua has changed at all.

Of course He has not. Yeshua is the same biblical and historical figure who walked and ministered in *Eretz Yisrael* nearly 20 centuries ago. It is our perception of Him that has changed so radically and so wrongly.

What are those forces that have clouded the true Yeshua? What has caused our *perception* of Him to have changed so drastically and so incorrectly?

UPROOTED!

First of all, through the centuries, Yeshua has undergone a process of being thoroughly "de-Judaized." He has literally been uprooted from His Jewish, biblical, and historical origins.

In almost every nation and country Yeshua has been taken in and adapted to that particular culture and society.

While that is not bad in one sense, what unfortunately has happened in the process is that the Jewish Jesus has been lost. The Jewish roots of this faith in Him have not been retained.

What began historically and biblically as a Jewish faith has been transformed in the years after His life into what is perceived today as a "non-Jewish" faith, with Yeshua Himself being perceived as being "non-Jewish."

In reality, though, Yeshua *was* a Jew.

In addition, all of His disciples were Jewish, as were the writers of the New Covenant and all of the apostles. In fact, this faith in Yeshua as the Messiah was for quite some time strictly a Jewish faith! It was not until later that the Gentiles were even allowed to come in!!!

Ironically, over the centuries, as this Jewish faith in Yeshua travelled from one culture to another, the Jewishness of Yeshua was lost.

What we are left with today is a paradoxical situation in which it is no longer considered Jewish to believe in Yeshua. Not so surprisingly, there are people today who are not even aware that Yeshua was a Jew!

In the past 2000 years or so, then, we have seen a definite "de-Judaizing" process, in which the Jewish Yeshua has been lost to the world.

RELIGIOSITY

The second great factor that has worked to cloud our perception of the true Yeshua is the presence of all the massive religious institutions that have sprung up around this Nazarene.

Yeshua has literally been enshrouded, engulfed and swept away in a tidal wave of religiosity that has been spawned by the trappings of this faith in Him. Services in His name overflow with rituals, traditions, great ceremony, pomp and splendor. There are hymns, songs, and chants in every language to Him, along with massive works of art. Even idols of gold and silver have been erected to Him.

A faith in Yeshua has produced infinite debates, massive theological works, seminaries, church councils, synods, schisms, and endless denominations.

No wonder it is so hard to find the real Yeshua!

One Jewish historian writes, "Through the thick cloud of religious incense, offered by the piety of countless generations, it is difficult to recognize the magnetic teacher of Galilee, who preached a gospel of love in an era filled with hate, whose simple humanity was a solace to those who lived in darkness."[1]

FROM THE MOONIES TO THE KKK

Finally, what also hinders us from clearly seeing Yeshua, is that everyone has used His name for whatever suited their needs, from the Gay Movement to Sun Myung Moon to the Ku Klux Klan.

Virtually every false prophet that has come along has used Yeshua's name in one way or another.

Wars have been fought, peoples persecuted and property confiscated in His name.

In addition to being misused, Yeshua's name has also been abused. He has been maligned, called traitor and false prophet. His name is even used today on the streets as a curse word!

Is it so unusual then that all this adds up to great confusion as to the historical Yeshua?

To truly understand this extraordinary person we need to set aside all of these cultural and religious barriers. We need to travel back in time and study Him in His environment, context and background. By seeing clearly where He lived, what He said, and to whom He said it, we can come to an understanding of what His goal and mission in life really were.

I can think of no better place to begin than with His very name, "Jesus," or as it is in Hebrew, "Yeshua."

4

From Jesus Christ to Yeshua Hamashiach

To most people in the world today, this man of Galilee is known as "Jesus Christ."

Yet this very name "Jesus Christ" is a classic example of how the Jewishness of Yeshua has been lost through the centuries.

YESHUA—HIS REAL NAME

Did you know that Yeshua never heard the name "Jesus" in his lifetime? When He was a boy growing up in Israel, His mother, father, brothers, sisters, and friends never called Him "Jesus" but "Yeshua" which is His actual Hebrew name.

The language of that day was not English but Hebrew or Aramaic, a closely related Semitic language.[1]

What does the name "Yeshua" actually mean?

Every time the Hebrew Scriptures use the word SALVATION (especially with the Hebrew suffix meaning "my," "thy," or "his"), with very few exceptions, it is absolutely the same identical word, YESHUA (Jesus).[2]

Most of the great men of God in the Bible had names with very special meanings, such as Daniel ("God is my Judge"), Ezekiel ("God Strengthens") and David ("Beloved"). In the same way, Yeshua's name has a special meaning, "Salvation."

According to the Brit Hadasha (the New Covenant), Yeshua was given this name when an angel appeared to His father,

Joseph, in a dream, saying, "And she [his wife, Miriam] shall bear a son, and you shall call His name Yeshua, for it is He who will save His people from their sins."[3]

"Yeshua," therefore means "Salvation" or "Savior." It was not an uncommon name in Israel at this time and was very similar to other names such as Joshua ("The Lord will Save"), Isaiah ("Salvation is of the Lord") and others.

Interestingly enough, the rabbis of old claimed that there were six whose names were given before birth: "Isaac, Ishmael, Moses, Solomon, Josiah and the name of the Messiah, whom may the Holy One, Blessed be His name, bring in our day."[4]

FROM YESHUA TO JESUS—HOW IT HAPPENED

The real name of "Jesus" then is "Yeshua." Our next step is to find out how the name of "Yeshua" became "Jesus."

In Yeshua's day, Greek was the *lingua franca* or the international language, much in the same way that English is today. As the faith in Yeshua spread throughout the Roman Empire, the Hebrew name "Yeshua" was translated into the Greek as "Iosous." Later "Iosous" was translated into English as "Jesus."

Obviously, for those who did not know the Hebrew origins of "Jesus," the meaning of His name along with the Jewish roots of His name were lost.

Therefore, "Jesus" is actually a hellenized-anglicized form of His Hebrew name, "Yeshua."

HEBREW	GREEK	ENGLISH
Yeshua	Iosous	Jesus

This does not mean that everyone should quit using the name "Jesus" today. Most people are quite comfortable with Yeshua's English name. He is certainly the same person whether His name is the Hebrew "Yeshua," the English "Jesus," or whatever it might be in Spanish, French, Russian or Chinese.

At the same time, it is important to know the Hebrew name of Jesus for a couple of reasons.

First of all, it is educational. This is His original name! This is the name which was given to Him at birth. This is the name by which His parents, family, friends, disciples, and followers in Israel called Him. This is the name which He had throughout His entire life!

Most scholars are constantly going back into the original languages of the Bible to better understand its inherent meaning (this is done with all ancient documents, for that matter).

How much more so with the very name of Yeshua!

It is important to know that His very name is "Salvation," and that this is why He came, i.e., to save His people from their sins.

Secondly, and more importantly, His Hebrew name helps us to put Yeshua back within His Jewish context and framework. The name "Yeshua" begins to restore the Jewish roots of this man and this faith in Him.

For just as His name has been hellenized and anglicized over the centuries, so the person of Yeshua has undergone the same treatment. Bringing back His original Hebrew name begins to put *Him* back within the proper biblical, cultural and national background from which He came.

FROM MESSIAH TO CHRIST—HOW IT HAPPENED

We cannot stop with just the name of Yeshua though. We also have to deal in the same manner with His "second name," "Christ."

Once again, we see the same kind of loss in the Jewish roots and meaning of this name.

Many people do not realize that "Christ" is not a second name like yours or mine, but is actually a title, like President, King or Prime Minister.

This extraordinary title originated in the Tenach* (Old Testament) as "Mashiach,"* which means in the Hebrew, "Anointed One."

---

*ch: Hebrew guttural sound.

Many men in the Bible were anointed by God's Spirit to serve Him, but gradually the writers of the Bible began to speak of a special "Anointed One" who would come and deliver Israel.

This title "Mashiach" or "Anointed One" eventually followed the same path that the Hebrew name Yeshua did, i.e., from the Hebrew into the Greek and then into English.

The early believers translated "Mashiach" from the Hebrew into the Greek "Christos," which also means "Anointed One" in that language. This was later translated into English as "Christ."

HEBREW	GREEK	ENGLISH
Mashiach	Christos	Christ

Once again, those who did not know the Jewish origins of the term "Christ" would not know that this was one of the greatest titles in the entire Bible given to the Deliverer and Savior of Israel.

Therefore, "Jesus Christ," literally in Hebrew is "Yeshua ha'Mashiach" or better translated into English without the Greek as "Yeshua the Messiah."

As in the case of the name "Jesus," it is certainly not wrong for anyone to use the term "Christ." However, it is still very important to know the origins of this title which is Jewish, and which carries such tremendous biblical and prophetic importance.

YESHUA IN THE TENACH (OLD TESTAMENT)

Can we find the name of "Jesus" or "Yeshua" anywhere in the Tenach?

The answer is, "Yes"!

"Yeshua" is not so easy to find until we realize that with very few exceptions, every time "Salvation" is mentioned in the Tenach, that this is "Yeshua" or a derivative form.

In a number of these places it is also quite clear that "salvation" refers to a Person and not to a Thing or an Event. In these contexts it *must* refer to the Messiah of Israel.

An outstanding example is found in the Book of Isaiah. In writing about Israel's future day of deliverance and salvation, Isaiah said, "Behold, the Lord has proclaimed to the end of the earth, say to the daughter of Zion, 'Lo, your Salvation comes; behold His reward is with Him, and His recompense before Him.'"[5]

Clearly, these statements show that the "Salvation" mentioned here is a Person and not a Thing or an Event to come. Who is this One? Obviously He is the One who will deliver Jerusalem and Israel. He is the Messiah of Israel, of whom the prophets spoke.[6]

Moving on to the Jewish prophet Habakkuk, we find another example.

In a great vision which this Jewish prophet received while in prayer, he saw God coming down to earth as a Warrior, to defend His people Israel from their enemies in the End of Days.

We read literally from the Hebrew "Thou wentest forth with YESHA (variant form of Yeshua) of thy people, with YESHA THY MESSIAH; you wound the head of the house of the Wicked One."[7]

Here is the very name of Yeshua accompanied by the title of Messiah or "Anointed One"!

So, for those who have always wondered why they have not been able to find the name of "Jesus" in the Tenach (Old Testament), here it is!!!

His actual name "Yeshua" is found throughout the Bible wherever "salvation" is used, particularly at those times when the context shows that "Salvation" is clearly a Person.

5

The New Covenant—
Myths and Legends?

To continue our search for the Jewish Yeshua, we must go back to the ancient sources of information that we have about Him.

Of course, our primary source of information is the "Brit Hadasha" (Hebrew for New Testament). Even more specifically, we are concerned with the first four books of the New Covenant (New Testament), which are four different accounts of Yeshua's life from four different perspectives.

These Jewish men all wrote their accounts in the 1st century A.D. Matai (Matthew in Hebrew) and Yohanan (John) were actually part of Yeshua's twelve disciples. Mark was a Messianic Jew of the 1st century who wrote his account a bit later as did Luke, a Jewish physician-historian.

In all likelihood, these four accounts were first written in Hebrew and later translated into Greek, to be dispersed throughout the Roman world.

Sometimes these four accounts are collectively called the "Gospels," from the Greek word meaning "Good News."

EVIDENCE FROM THE FIRST CENTURY

A theory has been floating around for a number of years that these four accounts were not written in the first century A.D., but were rather transmitted orally by Yeshua's disciples until about the 4th century A.D., when they were finally written down.

By this time, so the theory goes, myths and legends had been built up around Yeshua and were now incorporated into His life history through the Gospels.

Therefore, it is said, the New Covenant (New Testament) account of the Bible is not so much an accurate historical assessment of Yeshua's life, but rather a bunch of mythical stories which we have to sift through in order to find the truth.

While this theory may sound good on paper, it does not really line up with the historical and archaeological evidence.

Each book of the New Covenant (just like the Old Covenant) was written separately, and then later was compiled with other books into complete manuscripts. The earliest complete New Covenant that we actually possess is from the 4th century A.D. (about 300 years after the time of Yeshua).

Less complete manuscripts date back as early as the end of the 2nd century A.D. or the early 3rd century A.D. We even have a fragment from the book of Yohanan (John) that dates to about 130 A.D., only about 100 years or so after Yeshua.[1]

Some historians even believe that they have found New Covenant fragments that date back to somewhere between 50 and 100 A.D.![2]

If this is true, then it is proof positive that the early Messianic Jews (Jewish believers in Yeshua) began to immediately record the events of Yeshua's ministry, probably even during His lifetime!

Therefore, there was no oral transmission and no 300 years in which myths and legends could crop up.

NOT 1300 YEARS LATER EITHER!

Just to put the historical accuracy of the New Covenant into proper perspective, it is interesting to read this quote from one of the foremost historians today on the New Covenant period:

> Perhaps we can appreciate how wealthy the New Testament is in manuscript attestation if we compare the textual material for other ancient historical works . . . *The History of Thucydides* (about 460–400 B.C.) is known to us from

eight manuscripts, the earliest belonging to around A.D. 900 . . . The same is true of *The History of Herodotus* (about 488–428 B.C.). Yet no classical scholar would listen to an argument that the authenticity of Herodotus or Thucydides is in doubt because the earliest manuscripts of their works which are of any use to us are over 1300 years later than the originals![3]

We may have fragments from the New Covenant that are in the very *century* that Yeshua lived, not 1300 years later as in these two cases!

I know that to some this talk of ancient history and archaeology can get a bit stuffy. At the same time, it is important to understand the integrity and accuracy of the New Covenant.

TACITUS, SUETONIUS AND JOSEPHUS

Outside of the New Covenant, Yeshua is also talked about quite a bit by secular historians.

These extra-biblical accounts are important too, because they confirm the existence of Yeshua, confirm the Gospel accounts and show the powerful impact Yeshua had not only in Jerusalem and Judea, but as a force that sent reverberations throughout the Roman Empire in the 1st century.

For instance, the Roman historian Tacitus mentions the persecution of these believers in Yeshua by the Emperor Nero when he made them the scapegoats for the great fire of Rome. He relates how the believers, already a great multitude, derive their name "from one Christus who was executed in the reign of Tiberius by the procurator of Judea, Pontius Pilate."[4]

Suetonius, another Roman historian and secretary to the Emperor Hadrian (117–138 A.D.), refers to Yeshua as one "Chrestus." He writes of problems that arose in Rome because of these people during the reign of the Emperor Claudius (41–57 A.D.).[5]

Without a doubt, the most extraordinary passage about Yeshua was written by Josephus, a Jewish historian in the 1st century.

Josephus was a native of Israel and a Pharisee who took a leading part in the war against Rome in 66 A.D. After he was taken prisoner by the Romans, he won favor of the Emperor and acted as interpreter during the siege of Jerusalem. He received Roman citizenship upon returning to Rome and devoted himself to literary work, writing a history of the Jewish people and their war with Rome. In his massive writings we find this startling passage about Yeshua:

> Now there was about this time, Yeshua a wise man, if it be lawful to call him a man, for he was a doer of wonderful works—a teacher of such men as receive the truth with pleasure. He drew over to him both many of the Jews and of the Gentiles. He was the Messiah and when Pilate, at the suggestion of the principal men amongst us had condemned him to the cross, those that loved him at the first, did not forsake him, for he appeared to them alive again the third day as the divine prophets had foretold these and ten thousand other wonderful things concerning him; and the tribe of believers so named after him are not extinct at this day.[6]

What a remarkable attestation to the life, ministry and career of Yeshua the Messiah!

6

The Jewish Jesus

He was not white, Anglo-Saxon, Chinese, Indonesian, French, Irish or American.

He did not have blue eyes, pale skin and a halo that followed Him around wherever He went.

Yeshua was Jewish!

YESHUA EVEN LOOKED JEWISH!

Born in a Jewish home and raised all His life in *Eretz Yisrael* (the land of Israel), Yeshua even looked Jewish for that day! This is clear from a story in the book of Yohanan (John). One day Yeshua stopped to get a drink of water from a well outside a Samaritan village.

The Samaritans were regarded by the Jewish people as their enemies. They were foreign settlers who were transplanted by the Assyrian Empire centuries before Yeshua's day. They had intermarried with the Israelites and began to mix paganism and idolatry with the Bible. Eventually they erected their own temple on Mt. Gerizim, north of Jerusalem.

As Yeshua sat by the well, a Samaritan woman came out to draw water from the well. Yeshua asked her for a drink and she replied "How is it that you being a Jew, ask drink of me, a woman of Samaria? For the Jews have no dealings with the Samaritans."[1]

What is interesting to note is that as soon as this woman saw Yeshua, she *knew* that He was Jewish and not Samaritan (nor any other nationality, for that matter).

Why? Because Yeshua *looked* Jewish!

His clothes, His language and even His physical appearance distinguished Him as being unmistakably Jewish for that day!

HIS APPEARANCE

Physically, Yeshua was neither black nor white. He was dark and swarthy with very Semitic-looking features like the rest of His countrymen.

As was the Jewish custom of that day, He would have shoulder length hair and a beard. He spoke not only Hebrew, but the more common language of the day, Aramaic.

"He would, we may safely assume, go about in the ordinary, although not in the more ostentatious, dress, worn by the Jewish teachers of Galilee . . . his feet were probably shod with sandals . . . his inner garment, close-fitting, and descended to his feet . . . it was without seam, woven from the top throughout . . . round the middle it would be fastened with a girdle. Over this inner garment, he would most probably wear the square outer garment, or Talit, with the customary fringes or four long white threads . . ."[2]

As to His headdress, we have no description of it but we may set it down as certain that no Jewish teacher would appear in public with his head uncovered.

He probably wore the customary white linen "sudarim," wound about the head as a turban, with the ends of it falling down over the neck.[3]

So if we were to be transported back in time and space to see Yeshua, we would see a very Jewish man. Someone who looked Jewish at first glance and undoubtedly someone very much like the rest of the rabbis of that day.

It is important to revive this Jewish image of Yeshua in order to continue to restore Him to His proper Jewish background.

Remember that we have had misperceptions of Yeshua for centuries. We have seen Yeshua adapted to nearly every nation on the earth, and in the process lose His Jewish identity, so to speak.

Now we are seeking to restore that biblical and historical truth.

NOT SOFT AND WEAK

In addition to His non-Jewish image, Yeshua has oftentimes been portrayed as someone soft, weak and effeminate.

Once again, nothing could be further from the truth.

Yeshua was the son of a carpenter, and a carpenter Himself.[4] His body was strong and used to hard labor. Being the oldest child of a large family, the responsibility for helping to support the family would have fallen upon His shoulders.

Some even think that His father, Joseph, may have died early in Yeshua's childhood, since there is no mention of him later on during Yeshua's ministry, as there is with His mother, sisters and brothers.

If so, then the job of supporting His family would have fallen completely upon Him, and He would have taken over the modest carpentry business that His father had in Nazareth.

We also see that Yeshua was not soft and weak during His ministry. He did not travel throughout the land in an air conditioned bus or drive around in His brand new sports coupe or catch the local subway.

Yeshua was used to walking for miles and miles on foot, using lonely, dusty and dangerous roads. He was at the mercy of the scorching sun, wild animals and highwaymen, not to mention snakes and scorpions.

It was Yeshua's custom to withdraw into the desert for prayer and fasting. When He did so, He would sleep on the ground, under the stars, exposed to the elements.

Every indication we have about Yeshua historically is that He was a strong, healthy man. He worked with His hands, walked for miles each day, preached to thousands for hours, slept on the ground and fasted and prayed for days on end.

A SPIRITUAL REVOLUTIONARY

Nor was His message soft and weak. While He did say to "turn the other cheek," it was this same Yeshua who went into the temple and overthrew the tables of moneychangers who were disgracing the house of God.

It was this same Yeshua who then took up a scourge of small cords or whip and drove these men out of the temple with their animals, standing guard and not allowing them to come back in![5]

It was this same Yeshua who stood up a short time later in Jerusalem and railed against religious hypocrisy of His day, as did the Jewish prophets of old.[6]

Yeshua bucked the establishment without fear for His life. He was a spiritual and moral revolutionary who was determined to bring His people back to their God.

Yeshua was *not* weak and effeminate, nor was His message. He was a powerful man with a mighty purpose, vision and calling from God.

This is the Jewish Jesus.

This is Yeshua of Nazareth. All of those other misperceptions are man's ideas and not what history and the Word of God tell us.

We need to get away from the multiplicity of cultural masks Yeshua has been forced to wear throughout the centuries and study the life of this man who claimed to be the long-promised Jewish Messiah of Israel.

7

Galilee of the Nations

The Jewish prophet Isaiah had once proclaimed centuries ago, that a "great light" would one day shine forth from Galilee upon the people living there. The reason? Because at that time a child would be born whose name would be called "Wonderful, Counsellor, the Mighty God, the Everlasting Father, the Prince of Peace"![1]

This great light was to be the Messiah.

GATEWAY TO THE WORLD

What an unusual land this Galilee was!

At the time of Yeshua, the land of Israel was divided by the Romans into three provinces, Judea, Samaria, and Galilee, which was the northernmost province.

Galilee was the gateway to the ancient world.

It had become a great commercial center because of a heavily used highway that ran through the land called "The Way of the Sea" (later called by the Romans the Via Maris). This road began in Egypt, wound along the Mediterranean coast, cut across Israel, on through Galilee and up into Syrian Damascus.

The land itself was one of the most beautiful areas in all of Israel, as it is today.

With an abundance of water through wells, rivers and springs, Galilee became famous in ancient times for its rich and fruitful soil. Grapes, pomegranates, olives, olive oil, wines, fishing industries and wheat fields all yielded such an abundance as to become virtually proverbial in Yeshua's day.

The agricultural wealth of Galilee was so great that the ancient rabbis maintained it was easier to support an entire legion there than to raise one child in the more barren country to the south.[2]

Altogether, the cost of living in Galilee was about one-fifth that of the rest of Judea, such was their prosperity.[3]

THE PEASANT FARMERS OF GALILEE

Galilee was most important, though, for its people.

Here is where the masses of Jewish people lived. Josephus estimated that there were about 240 towns and villages of Galilee each with not less than 15,000 inhabitants. He estimated Galilee's total population at about 3 million![4]

While this may be an exaggeration, we have in Galilee all the conditions necessary for the support of a numerous and prosperous people. This helps us to understand the crowds of people that gathered around and followed Yeshua in this district, where the greatest part of His public life was spent. That the Jewish population in the centuries immediately following Yeshua was numerous and wealthy is proved by the remains of those times, especially the ruins of synagogues.[5]

The peasant farmers of Galilee were a bold and enterprising lot. They were warm, simple, generous, impulsive, pious, excitable, passionate, and violent. While the Talmud accused them of being quarrelsome, it also admits that they cared more for honor than money.[6]

The Galileans were also simpler in their faith than the religious establishment in Jerusalem. They were inclined to be more mild and rational in their application of traditionalism.

As a result, they were looked down upon by the religious hierarchy of Jerusalem, who scorned them for neglecting the traditions and for being unable to rise to its great speculative heights.[7]

They were also looked down upon for neglecting the study of their own language, and were ridiculed for their peculiar dialect which was easily distinguishable.

A HOTBED OF REBELLION

Finally, and possibly most importantly, the Galileans were intensely nationalistic and patriotic.

They were a thorn in the side of their Roman overlords and were a constant hotbed of rebellion. They were ready to fight at a moment's notice and hated the Romans with a passion.

Eventually, out of Galilee arose a fanatically anti-Roman society called the Zealots, whose nationalistic fire and violence eventually led to outright war with Rome in 66 A.D.

Any military leader claiming to be the Messiah and Savior of Israel had a quick and warm reception in Galilee!

It was here that the Messianic Hope was the greatest, as the people looked fervently and desperately for that One who would come and throw off the yoke of the hated Romans, ushering in an era of peace and tranquility for the entire world.

8

As a Child

It was in this rich and colorful environment that Yeshua was raised as a child.

We know very little about the childhood and upbringing of Yeshua. Even the Gospel records are strangely silent in this area.

Undoubtedly, the early Messianic writers of the New Covenant did not want later generations to distort and uplift His childhood with silly fables and legends (which some eventually did anyway).

Despite this lack of information, we can still get a pretty good idea of what life must have been like for Yeshua as a child. We get such a picture through our historical knowledge of that period in Israel and from the bit of information we can glean from the New Covenant about Yeshua's early life.

CIRCUMCISED ON THE EIGHTH DAY

Yeshua was born in Bethlehem, a little town six miles south of Jerusalem. He was born here because the Romans were taking a census, and all of the Jewish people had to return to their hometowns. Since Yeshua's parents, Joseph and Miriam, were of the tribe of Judah, and the royal seed of David, they had to return to Bethlehem and stay until the census was over.

It was in this birthplace of King David that Yeshua was born.

We know that on the 8th day this child was circumcised in accordance with the Law of Moses, and named "Yeshua" which means "Salvation."[1]

Also in accordance with the Law of Moses, Yeshua was taken to the temple in Jerusalem after 40 days to be presented before the Lord as the first-born.[2]

Eventually, this tiny family went back to Galilee, to their own city of Nazareth, and settled there. It was in this little town by the Sea of Galilee that Yeshua was raised as a child.

He learned the trade of His father and became a carpenter.

Yeshua also received a good education, for later we find that He could read and write well in both Hebrew and Aramaic, the common language of that day in Israel.[3]

SPIRITUAL TRAINING

As for the spiritual and biblical training of this child, once again we can deduce certain things from history and the Word of God.

Since there was a synagogue in Nazareth at this time, undoubtedly Yeshua went with His father every Shabbat (Sabbath).

In all likelihood there was a school attached to the synagogue, as this was the custom. In this school Yeshua would have read Moses and the Prophets. After the reading, the rabbis would give a discourse in much the same manner as Yeshua would give later in His life.

The real spiritual training, though, came in the home through His parents. Joseph and Miriam were devout Jews with a great love for the God of Abraham, Isaac and Jacob.

Just as in every Jewish home at this time, Yeshua was taught to keep all the great festivals in the Bible, such as Passover, Shavuot (the Feast of Weeks), Yom Kippur (the Day of Atonement), Sukkot (the Feast of Booths), Hanukkah, Purim and many others.

These festivals would obviously have a great impact upon any child's mind, as they read and studied the Tenach (Old Covenant) concerning Israel's extraordinary relationship with God.

At this time, we know that almost every home in Israel possessed at least a portion of the Tenach. They were in the form of scrolls written out on parchment or Egyptian paper. There were even little parchment rolls for the use of the children which contained biblical passages such as the "Shema" (Deuteronomy 6:4–9), the Hallel Psalms (113–118) and the history of creation to the flood.[4]

So we know that Yeshua had tremendous access to the Word of God and this coupled with being under the tutelage of His godly parents, He grew in His love for Israel, the God of Abraham, Isaac and Jacob, and the Holy Scriptures.

MISSING IN JERUSALEM

We have but one incident in the entire New Covenant concerning Yeshua's early years. One incident in which God peels back the curtain of silence to let us catch a glimpse at the progress of this extraordinary child.

His parents, Joseph and Miriam, were going up to Jerusalem for the Feast of Passover as they did every year.

Attendance at all the major festivals (Passover, Shavuot or the Feast of Weeks, and Sukkot or the Feast of Booths) was required in the Law of Moses. While the Jewish people in the Diaspora would have a hard time making these three festivals, devout Jewish people like Joseph and Miriam faithfully made the pilgrimage to Jerusalem.

When Yeshua turned twelve, they took Him on their annual trip to Jerusalem for Passover.

Some have thought that on this occasion, Yeshua went up to Jerusalem for His "Bar Mitzvah." This term means "son of the commandment" and is a time when every Jewish male comes "of age;" when he becomes responsible for religious obligations and privileges. This is also when he becomes a member of the synagogue.

While undoubtedly Yeshua did become a "son of the commandment" and did go through this procedure, it was not at this time. The age of "Bar Mitzvah" is 13 and not 12.

Since the training for this ceremony usually begins a year and sometimes two years ahead of time, Yeshua was probably going up to Jerusalem in preparation for becoming a "son of the commandment."[5]

When Passover was completed, Joseph and Miriam left for home.

Since everyone travelled in a large caravan for protection at this time, the small children and women went ahead followed by the bigger boys and men. In this great throng of people, Joseph and Miriam suddenly realized that Yeshua was missing.

They returned to Jerusalem and finally discovered Him in the temple ". . . sitting in the midst of the teachers both listening to them, and asking them questions. And all who heard Him were amazed at His understanding and His answers."[6]

When questioned anxiously by His parents about His disappearance, He replied, "Why is it that you were looking for Me? Did you not know that I had to be in My Father's house?"[7]

Nevertheless, despite His great zeal for spiritual matters, Yeshua returned with His parents to Nazareth and submitted to them.

What this one incident shows us is that very early in His life, Yeshua had a vision and understanding of what His purpose in life was to be. He also displayed a great hunger for spiritual issues and such a grasp of the Scriptures that it amazed the rabbis in Jerusalem.

"And Yeshua kept increasing in wisdom and stature, and in favor with God and men."[8]

Yeshua continued on this spiritual path of teaching and biblical training, becoming a very popular teacher and expounder of the Scriptures in Galilee.

9

Messiahs, Messiahs, Messiahs!

As a child, Yeshua grew up in one of the most crucial and dramatic periods in Israel's history.

It was a period of chaos, growing disillusionment and fear. Events were leading up to what would prove to be the final years of Israel's national existence for nearly 1900 years.

Before the turn of the century, the People of the Book would be scattered to the four corners of the earth in worldwide dispersion and chaos, thus beginning their long odyssey away from the homeland that God had given to them.

This national destruction would come at the hands of the largest and most powerful empire the world had seen to date ... the Roman Empire.

THE IRON BEAST

Ever since the 8th century B.C., Israel had been overrun by one foreign army after another. Just like the rest of the nations around them, they were incorporated into each particular empire for a period of time.

First came the Assyrians, who destroyed the northern nation of Israel, comprised of the ten tribes, and then subjugated the southern nation of Judah for a time.

After the Assyrians came the Babylonians in the 6th century B.C., who with a cruelty unparalleled, destroyed the temple, razed Jerusalem to the ground, and carried off the Jewish people into captivity for 70 years.

Yet Israel survived.

They returned when King Cyrus of Persia defeated the Babylonians and allowed the Jewish people to return to their land. The nation of Israel existed as a part of this mostly benevolent Persian Empire for nearly two centuries.

Then came Alexander the Great.

Sweeping out of the West, he descended upon the Persian Empire and destroyed them with a vengeance. Upon Alexander's death his huge empire was divided among his four generals. Once again Israel was under foreign domination, this time coming primarily from Syria.

For a brief span of about 100 years, the nation of Israel, under the leadership of the Maccabees, was able to throw off this foreign yoke and live under self-rule.

But then came the Romans.

These conquerors were characterized by the Jewish prophet Daniel many centuries earlier as a dreadful and terrible Beast, exceedingly strong with teeth of iron that ripped its prey to shreds with cold and brutal efficiency.[1]

During this period, the Romans were truly invincible. They had an empire that stretched from northern Africa to Britain, from the Euphrates River to the Atlantic Ocean and from the Caucasus Mountains in Russia to the Nile River deep in the heart of Egypt.

Now it was Israel's turn to deal with the Romans.

PANGS OF THE MESSIAH

From the very beginning, the presence of the Romans in the land of Israel was an offense to the Jewish people.

One reason was because Israel had enjoyed nearly 100 consecutive years of independence under the royal family, the Maccabees. Now, suddenly, that freedom was taken away by a powerful, inflexible and oppressive overlord.

There were also constant clashes over the issues of religion. The Romans were insensitive to the Jewish faith, considering Judaism barbaric and backward. On the other hand, the Jewish people considered the Romans heathens and pagans, especially despising their cultic emperor worship.

All too often, the Romans tactlessly overstepped their bounds and offended the Jewish nation in regards to their faith.

In addition, the Romans taxed the province of Judea mercilessly. Israel, at this time, was mostly agricultural, and the land had a limited yield. Under the tremendous pressure of the Roman Empire, the peasant population was being taxed into abject poverty.

To make matters worse, many of the Roman officials were corrupt, taking bribes and "squeezing" the people for as much money as they could get.

"The officials of the Roman provinces are like flies on a sore but those already sated with blood do not suck so hard as the newcomers."[2]

Added to all this was an onslaught of catastrophes that included an earthquake, crop failures, famine and plague all within just a short period of time. It was no wonder that the nation of Israel listened with awe to the words of self-appointed prophets who proclaimed that these trials were but the "pangs of the Messiah" that would introduce the end of the world.

MACCABEES, ZEALOTS & SICARRII

Soon the land of Israel became a seething cauldron of rebellion.

Ever since the days of the Maccabees, great fighters who delivered the Jewish people out of the hands of their oppressors in 165 B.C., a fierce national spirit had developed in Israel.

Now, any number of impetuous young men, hoping to duplicate the achievements of the Maccabees, retired to the hills of Judea and Galilee, emerging from their hiding places to attack stray Roman contingents, or such Jews as had made their peace with Rome. The Jewish people looked on these valiant, hopeful dreamers as patriots, while the Romans looked upon them as highwaymen and murderers.[3]

Out of Galilee arose Rome's most serious opponent, the Zealots, of whom one of Yeshua's 12 closest disciples was once a member. These fiery patriots were avowed to Jewish independence from Roman rule at any cost.

Even more ominous were the Sicarrii, or "wielders of the dagger." They were assassins who murdered pro-Roman priests and Jewish aristocrats sympathetic to the Romans, even carrying out their attacks within the temple precinct.

"Ultimately Roman patience was thoroughly exhausted and the procurators introduced measures of barbarous severity. Soldiers slew on the slightest provocation. Eminent Jewish leaders were crucified, whole villages were razed. All in vain. A fever of martyrdom seemed to seize upon the harassed people. Fanatics went up and down the country, wild-eyed and frantic, prophesying the end of the world and the advent of the Messiah. Multitudes were ready to follow every impossible visionary who claimed inspiration from heaven. Zealots rushed to their death crying out in hysterical exaltation."[4]

There was only one Person who could deliver Israel from this ever-worsening crisis. Only one Person could defeat the Romans and bring salvation to Israel.

All of Israel was frantically waiting for the Messiah to appear.

AN ERA OF MESSIANIC FERVOR

Into this swirling maelstrom of political and religious activity, a Messianic fervor was born within the Jewish people.

The concept of a great Deliverer and Savior of Israel was over a millenium old in the conscience of the Chosen People. Scripture passages about the Messiah extended back into the Torah and continued right on into the writings of the Jewish prophets of Isaiah, Jeremiah, Daniel, Ezekiel, Zechariah and many others.

But never was the Messianic expectation and desire as great as now.

Because of Israel's great oppressions and seemingly hopeless future, the populace looked desperately for the Anointed One.

Surely, He had to come now, with the ever-worsening economic condition, famine, earthquakes and their terrible overlord, Rome.

So, the people cast their eye about frantically looking for the Messiah to arise from their midst and deliver the Chosen People once and for all.

Every wild-eyed fanatic claiming to be the prophet of God was proclaimed Messiah and followed by some segment of the population.

False messiahs abounded. Apocalyptic literature about the "End of Days" proliferated. Sects appeared, living in the desert or some other isolated spot. Severing all ties with the normal world and living ascetic lifestyles, they waited patiently for the coming of the Messiah and the era of peace and prosperity that would be ushered in.

A MILITARY MESSIAH

Most of all, the masses were looking for a "military" Messiah; someone who would come with a great army and throw off the terrible yoke of Roman oppression.

Israel desperately wanted a man to arise who would lead them against their hated enemies; someone who would defeat their enemies and set up His eternal kingdom of peace as the prophets of old had predicted.

While the prophets did speak of the Messiah coming and delivering Israel from their enemies and setting up a Kingdom of Peace, they also spoke of a completely different role the Messiah would have to play.

They spoke of this great King coming in humility and meekness. He would not immediately destroy Israel's enemies and judge the earth. Instead, he would come to suffer and die for the sins of His people.

The Jewish prophet Isaiah said, "All of us like sheep have gone astray, Each of us has turned to his own way; But the Lord has caused the iniquity of us all to fall on Him."[5]

These "Suffering Messiah" passages were recognized by the rabbis in the first century as being truly Messianic. While the rabbis and the people in Israel may not have fully understood what these scriptures meant, without a doubt, they did recognize that the Messiah had to suffer for our sins.

In fact, there are really more passages that speak of this Suffering Messiah than of the Conquering Messiah!

NO NEED FOR A SUFFERING MESSIAH

But, with the political situation growing worse day by day and the catastrophies seeming to multiply upon the land, the consciousness of the Suffering Messiah grew ever fainter.

A Suffering Messiah was not needed nor even particularly desired. How could such a one defeat the Romans? How could such a one cause murder and strife to cease? How could such a Messiah heal the land and stop famine from occurring?

Obviously, the Conquering Messiah became the popular view in Israel, as a parade of one military Messiah after another tried their luck against the Romans.

All to no avail.

Only a handful were still looking for a Messiah who would come in humility and die for their sins. Only a remnant was looking for one who could deliver not only from the Romans but also from sin, unrighteousness and condemnation.

They were not disappointed.

10

Yeshua the Rabbi

At this critical juncture in Israel's history, Yeshua began His great career.

In just three short years, this carpenter from Galilee would change the course of human history for the next twenty centuries.

Who was this Yeshua of Nazareth? What did He do that made Him so great? How could one man affect world history more powerfully than any other before Him?

WITH POWER AND AUTHORITY

One of Yeshua's talents that effected such a tremendous impact in Israel was His great teaching ability. Yeshua was one of Israel's greatest rabbis of that day.

While sometimes His great healings and miracles are most often associated with His name, Yeshua actually spent more time teaching the Word of God than anything else.

Yeshua taught His people from the Holy Scriptures, proclaiming that the Kingdom of God is at hand, seeking to bring them into a deeper understanding and commitment to the God of Abraham, Isaac and Jacob.

Although He was a simple Galilean carpenter who did not "graduate" from any of the traditional rabbinic schools, Yeshua was considered a great Teacher by the people.

He began His ministry at the age of 30 and continued for three years. He taught first in His native Galilee and then later in Jerusalem.

Yeshua taught everywhere that He could, including in synagogues, in village squares, on streetcorners, in the countryside, from hilltops and even from boats, while the masses sat on the shore and listened.

He must have had a powerful voice to speak to so many thousands at one time without the use of any kind of modern sound equipment!

The people flocked to Him in droves. For when Yeshua spoke, it was with unusual power and authority. On one occasion when Yeshua had finished speaking, ". . . the multitudes were amazed at His teaching; for He was teaching them as one having authority, and not as their scribes."[1]

One Jewish scholar and historian said this concerning Yeshua's teaching: ". . . the manner in which [Yeshua] ministered was unique. Few had ever prayed and taught with such charm and power. His radiant personality, his tenderness, and humility, captivated the masses wherever he went, and inspired confidence. As a teacher, he was superb. He had the divine gift of a lucid tongue and a colorful imagination. His parables, pregnant with thought and rich with spiritual meaning, were yet simple enough for a child to follow. When he spoke, men listened enthralled and begged for his blessing. Faith in his power to heal may have relieved many who were afflicted, and the word spread through the countryside that a new prophet had arisen, the magic of whose touch restored the blind and animated the halt."[2]

PARABLES

Yeshua taught strictly out of the Word of God: the Torah (the first five books of Moses), the Ketiviim (the historical and political books) and the Neviim (the Prophets).

Yeshua often taught using a unique device called a "parable." A parable is a story or illustration taken from the common daily life in order to teach a spiritual truth or principle. The meaning might be immediately clear, or it might take some studying and meditating in order to understand.

Yeshua had an unusual variety of parables.

For instance, He once likened the "Kingdom of Heaven" to ". . . a treasure hidden in the field, which a man found and hid; and from joy over it he goes and sells all that he has, and buys that field. Again, the Kingdom of Heaven is like a merchant seeking fine pearls, and upon finding one pearl of great value, he went and sold all that he had and bought it."[3]

In other words, this parable taught that to become a part of God's Kingdom is so precious that it is like possessing a valuable pearl or treasure. It is such a great blessing that God becomes first and foremost in our lives. He becomes that great treasure, that priceless pearl to us.

Another parable Yeshua taught was that of "The Sower and the Seed."

He said that the Word of God is like a seed that is sown in our hearts. Sometimes the seed falls by the wayside and is lost. Sometimes the seed falls on stony places and is received for a time, but there is no deep root in the heart and it eventually dies. Sometimes the seed falls among thorns and is choked by the cares of the world. But sometimes, Yeshua taught, the seed is sown in "good ground" and is received. That person turns their heart to God and begins to live for Him in their lives.[4]

Yeshua spoke in parables to make his teachings easier for the average person to understand and to relate to. His teaching was not for scholars lost in their ivory towers, but for the masses to know God more deeply.

Oftentimes, Yeshua did not want the meaning of his parable to be immediately clear. He wanted his disciples and the people to think and meditate upon the Word of God so that it would sink deep into their hearts and become real to them personally.

A BOLD NEW CONCEPT OF LOVE

While Yeshua taught from the Scriptures, He oftentimes introduced bold, new ideas and concepts, as did the Jewish prophets before Him and the rabbis of that day.

One of His most famous teachings was on the topic of "love," ironically given in such a period of hate, strife and turmoil.

When asked one day, what was the greatest commandment in

the Law, Yeshua replied, "You shall love the Lord your God with all your heart, and with all your soul, and with all your mind. This is the great and foremost commandment. The second is like it, 'You shall love your neighbor as yourself.' On these two commandments depend ᴛɦe whole Law ᴀnd Prophets."[5]

On another occasion Yeshua undoubtedly shocked the multitudes when he stated, "But I say to you, love your enemies, and pray for those who persecute you, in order that you may be sons of your Father who is in heaven. . ."[6]

And of course, Yeshua taught what is commonly called today, "The Golden Rule," "Therefore, however you want people to treat you, so treat them, for this is the Law and the Prophets."[7]

A NEW HEART

This great teacher, Yeshua, taught the people how to pray, how to have a personal walk with God, and how to have a love for the Word of God.

Yeshua taught on just about every subject imaginable, including adultery, lust, divorce, perjury, revenge, money, fasting, prayer, the Shabbat, the Spirit of God, and prophetic events that were to come upon the earth.

He taught from almost every book in the Tenach and used most of the great characters familiar to the people, such as Elijah, Moses, Jonah, Daniel and many others.

Perhaps Yeshua's greatest teaching of all though was on the heart, the seat of our emotions, and wherein lies our very soul. "For the mouth speaks out of that which fills the heart. The good man out of his good treasure brings forth what is good; and the evil man out of his evil treasure brings forth what is evil."[8]

Yeshua was not concerned with outward appearances of righteousness (any more than God is today).

Rules and rituals are fine, but God loves a contrite and humble spirit. God desires a true love for Him that comes from the heart.

"Do not lay up for yourselves treasures upon earth, where moth and rust destroy, and where thieves break in and steal. But lay up for yourselves treasures in heaven . . . *for where your treasure is, there will your heart be also.*"[9]

Yeshua taught that God demands more than an outward show of religiosity. God wants our hearts to be right with Him.

To turn to God and to live for Him day by day was the primary concern of Yeshua the Rabbi.

11

Israel's Greatest Prophet

To say that Yeshua was simply a great rabbi or teacher would not be sufficient to do Him justice.

He did not claim to be *just* a teacher, nor was He perceived by the people to be merely a teacher. Yeshua was considered a great *prophet* sent by God to Israel.

We find in the New Covenant, after one particular miracle in Yeshua's ministry, that "fear gripped them [Israel] all, and they began glorifying God, saying, 'A great prophet has arisen among us!' and, 'God has visited His people [Israel]!'"[1]

Therefore, in addition to being a great rabbi, Yeshua was also a prophet, actually the greatest prophet in Israel's long history.

THE RISE OF THE PROPHETS

Truly, prophecy is proof of the divine inspiration of Scripture. For who else can correctly foretell the future? Who can inerrantly predict events that will come true centuries before they occur?

Only God and His messengers, to whom He is revealing this information here on this earth. These messengers were the Jewish prophets.

Almost from the beginning of Israel's history as a nation there were prophets.

They were an extraordinary group of men dedicated to God. Boldly proclaiming their message to their people, they made predictions which only God could know.

For example, Jeremiah predicted the 70 years of captivity that Israel would have to spend in Babylon, many years before the Babylonians ever invaded the land.[2] Isaiah spoke of the Persian King Cyrus some 200 years before Cyrus was even born![3] Daniel vividly described the invasion of Alexander the Great and the Roman Empire which would follow, centuries before either of these nations was even a world power![4]

THE CONSCIENCE OF THE PEOPLE

There was no prophetic lineage that spawned a class or genealogy of prophets. These men were all called out individually and supernaturally by God.

They came from a variety of backgrounds ranging from shepherds and farmers, to priests and royalty.

Men such as Isaiah, Jeremiah, Ezekiel, Daniel, Moses, David, Elijah, Nathan, Jonah and Zechariah were just a few such men who shaped and guided the course of Jewish history for thousands of years.

Some lived ascetic lifestyles in the desert or mountains. Here they would fast and pray for long periods of time, visiting the people only when they had a message from God.

Others lived among the people, guiding them day by day with their teaching and giving counsel to the rulers of the land.

The prophets were the conscience of the people.

Fiery orators imbued with the power of the *Ruach HaKodesh* (the Holy Spirit), they were completely sold out to the God of Abraham, Isaac and Jacob. They would brook no compromise with idolatry, false gods or heathenism in any form.

Oftentimes they were the leaders of a fragile remnant still loyal to God, while at other times they led great national revivals and established schools of prophets throughout the land.

They proclaimed their message on street corners, in the bazaars, in the temple, at the king's palace, or in the countryside, wherever they could get the attention of the people.

No one escaped their sometimes scathing rebuke when they detected hypocrisy and spiritual adultery against the God of Israel.

Not all of their prophecies were predictive. In fact, the majority of their messages were exhortative, encouraging, and, when necessary, chastising, in order to get their people right with God.

They railed against the priests, Levites, kings and authorities for forsaking their God, risking their lives in the process. Many of them actually died for their faith.

PROPHETIC ARTISTS

Most of the Jewish prophets committed their prophecies to writing, either at their own hand or with the help of an assistant.

Prophets like Isaiah, Ezekiel and Jeremiah were prolific writers. Others such as Joel, Hosea and Amos wrote short but powerful essays. Some of the greatest prophets though, such as Elijah and Elisha, left no written word at all.

It is particularly those prophets who recorded their divinely inspired messages who are important to us today.

For these 20–25 prophetic artists painted an harmonious picture that lasted over a period of thousands of years. Their predictions for the future were remarkably consistent concerning their land, their people, and the world.

Especially in regard to the coming Messiah and the era of peace that He would usher in, the Jewish prophets were united in one accord.

HOW TO TEST A PROPHET

The Torah outlines the tests for a prophet to see if he is truly of God or not. First of all, his prophecies quite simply *all* had to come true. If they did not, he was considered to be a false prophet and stoned to death by the people.[5]

The second test was if his words and teachings were in accordance with the Word of God. If he said to go after other gods and taught the people contrary to the Law, then he was a false prophet.[6]

It did not make any difference whether he did miracles or not. A true prophet's ministry was to be founded upon the

Word of God, and he must lead the people toward God and not away from Him.

While false prophets abounded, it was this extraordinary group of *true* prophets who were God's primary tool in guiding Israel for over fifteen centuries.

THE DISAPPEARANCE

Then the Jewish prophets disappeared. After the return of Israel from the Babylonian captivity in the 6th century B.C., the prophetic ministry began to fade in Israel.

Malachi was the last Jewish prophet, writing and preaching around 440 B.C. After him came silence for nearly 400 years. No prophet appeared during this time to give Israel God's prophetic word.

Finally, after 400 years a prophet did appear.

Not Yeshua, but a man named Yohanan the Immerser. He was given that name because he immersed people in water as a sign of moral and spiritual purification from their sins (in agreement with the Torah).

Truly, Yohanan came in the spirit of the prophets of old! Wearing a garment of camel's hair and a leather belt about his waist, his food consisted of only locusts and wild honey.

Despite his wild appearance and lifestyle, the people responded to his powerful message of repentance. They came out in droves to the Jordan River to repent of their sins and get right with God.

Yohanan did not consider himself to be a teacher so much as someone ordained by God to prepare the way for the Messiah.

He said, "After me One is coming who is mightier than I, and I am not fit to stoop down and untie the thong of His sandals. I (immersed) you with water; but He will (immerse) you with the Holy Spirit."[7]

The one of whom Yohanan was speaking was the same one that Moses spoke of centuries before when he said, "The Lord your God will raise up for you a Prophet like me from among you, from your countrymen, you shall listen to Him . . . and

[God said] I will put My words in His mouth, and He shall speak to them all that I command Him. And it shall come about that whoever will not listen to My words which He shall speak in My name, I Myself will require it of him.''[8]

Moses knew that there would be many prophets who would come after him. He was speaking about a special one who would come, the greatest prophet Israel would ever see.

YESHUA'S PREDICTIONS

Into this long and rich history of prophets, from Moses to Yohanan, came Yeshua.

Truly, Yeshua had all the characteristics of a great prophet. His predictions were some of the boldest and most accurate in all of Israel's history.

He spoke of events that were to come upon the land in that very century. In particular, He perfectly described the destruction of the temple and the terrible invasion by the Romans that occurred in 70 A.D.

In addition, Yeshua predicted of events that would occur in the far distant future. He spoke of the ''Last Days'' and ''End-times of this Age.''

''And there will be signs in sun and moon and stars, and upon the earth dismay among nations, in perplexity at the roaring of the sea and the waves, men fainting from fear and the expectation of the things which are coming upon the world; for the powers of the heavens will be shaken. And then they will see the Son of Man coming in a cloud with power and great glory. But when these things begin to take place, straighten up and lift up your heads, because your redemption is drawing near.''[9]

Yeshua spoke extensively about this period of great tribulation that would come upon the earth, the rise of the Anti-Messiah, the sun becoming black, the moon turning to blood, and other cataclysmic events that would take place on the earth.

But He also spoke of the Son of Man coming in power and glory to defeat the enemies of Israel, to judge the nations and to usher in an era of peace and harmony throughout the world.

ATTACKING THE ESTABLISHMENT

Just as with the Jewish prophets before Him, Yeshua did not spend the majority of His time making predictions.

A prophet is more than a seer. He is a messenger sent from God to bring the people back to God.

So Yeshua encouraged, exhorted, chastised and rebuked whenever necessary.

If there was a difference between Yeshua's message and that of His predecessors, it was that while their major battle was against idolatry, His was against a religious establishment that had arisen and had strayed far from God.

A contemporary Jewish historian says of that period, "Unfortunately the time was out of joint for the liberalism of (Yeshua). Many of the men whom he encountered were Pharisees who mistook the inner meaning of Pharisaism. For them the ideal of a life consecrated by religious rites, a life in which every step, from the eating of a meal to the wearing of a new cloak, was a sacred act, had degenerated into a blind, fanatical adherence to forms. This type had been denounced far back in the 8th century B.C. The Talmud contains many bitter protests against 'making the law a burden,' against 'laws that hang on hairs', against wicked priests and Pharisees."[10]

It was against this religious establishment and aristocracy that Yeshua fought. He saw their hypocrisy and chastised the leaders to get right with God.

Finally, in one of His greatest confrontations with the establishment, Yeshua cried out, "Woe to you, scribes and Pharisees, hypocrites! For you are like whitewashed tombs, which on the outside appear beautiful, but inside they are full of dead men's bones, and all uncleanness. Even so you too outwardly appear righteous to men, but inwardly you are full of hypocrisy and lawlessness."[11]

IS THE NEW COVENANT ANTI-SEMITIC?

Sometimes people read these denouncements by Yeshua and conclude that the New Covenant is anti-Semitic.

Nothing could be further from the truth!

Yeshua was exercising his God-given right and calling as a prophet, to expose, denounce and preach *against sin.*

What Yeshua said in the New Covenant is certainly no different than what we find the Jewish prophets saying in the Tenach. In fact, sometimes their attack on kings, priests and religious leaders of the day was far worse than anything Yeshua ever said!

Ezekiel said, "Prophesy against the shepherds of Israel. Woe, shepherds of Israel who have been feeding themselves! Should not the shepherds feed the flock?"[12] Jeremiah cried out, "Woe to the shepherds who are destroying and scattering the sheep of My pasture!"[13] Isaiah challenged, "Hear the word of the Lord, You rulers of Sodom; give ear to the instruction of our God, you people of Gomorrah."[14]

That is the role of a prophet, to fight sin and hypocrisy and lead the people back to God.

Yeshua rebuked the nation and their leaders out of love for His God and His people. To the Jewish prophet, any religion created by man is an abomination to God. All of man's clever theology, incantations, and giant, sparkling, spiritually-sterile buildings are rejected by God.

"Who can enter the mountain of the Lord," the Psalmist asks. "Who can stand in His holy hill? He who has clean hands and a pure heart."

That is the role of the Jewish prophet in the Bible, to get the heart of the people back to God. That was Yeshua's concern as he rose to become the greatest prophet in the history of his people.

12

When the Messiah *Had* to Come

Once again we cannot stop with Yeshua being just another prophet any more than we could stop with Him being just another teacher or rabbi.

Yeshua himself claimed to be far more than a prophet.

He said, "I am the way, and the truth, and the life; no one comes to the Father, but through Me . . . I am in the Father, and the Father is in Me . . . If you love me, you will keep My commandments."[1]

These are pretty strong words for just a prophet!

When asked by the High Priest if He was the Messiah, Yeshua replied, "I am, and you shall see the Son of Man sitting at the right hand of power, and coming with the clouds of heaven."[2]

So Yeshua claimed to be more than just a teacher or a prophet. He claimed to be the Messiah of Israel, of whom the Law and the Prophets foretold.

THE PROPHETIC PICTURE OF THE MESSIAH

The purpose of this book is not to go through all of the Messianic passages in the Tenach to prove that Yeshua is the Messiah.

You can do that for yourself.

All you have to do is study the Scriptures and see if Yeshua's life lines up with the Word of God, provided, of course, that you study the Word of God with an open and objective mind.

No one passage will answer all of your questions. But, as you piece together this centuries-long, prophetic puzzle, you will see that there is only one possible person who could have fulfilled all of the prophecies, and that is Yeshua of Nazareth.

"Who could draw a picture of a man not yet born? Surely God, and God alone. Nobody knew 500 years ago that Shakespeare was going to be born; or 250 years ago that Napoleon was to be born. Yet here in the Bible we have the most striking and unmistakeable likeness of a man portrayed, not by one, but by twenty-five artists, none of whom have ever seen the man they have been painting."[3]

PROPHECY OF THE 70 WEEKS

While we do not have the time or space here to go through all of the Messianic prophecies, one in particular is of great importance to us because it gives the *TIME* when the Messiah *had to* come.

This extraordinary prediction is found in the 9th chapter of Daniel and is oftentimes called "The Prophecy of the Seventy Weeks" (i.e., 70 weeks of years or 490 years).

When you study this remarkable prophecy in its context, it gives the exact date of when the Messiah was to appear!

To fully understand this prediction we need to know a little bit of its background.

The Jewish prophet Daniel lived in the 6th century B.C. It was in this crucial century that the Babylonians invaded the land of Israel. They destroyed Solomon's temple, burned the city of Jerusalem to the ground and took all of the people captive to Babylon for 70 years. After 70 years the Persians, under King Cyrus, defeated the Babylonians and allowed the Jewish people to return to their homeland.

Daniel was one of the Jewish captives originally taken to Babylon. Because of his intelligence and royal lineage, he was placed in the palace to study and be trained to serve the king. Eventually he rose to a position of great prominence in the king's court.

One day, while fasting and praying about Israel's return to

the land, an angel appeared to him and gave him a prophecy about Israel's future.

He told Daniel that the Jewish people would definitely return to their land shortly and that the city of Jerusalem would be rebuilt. Included in this prophecy of Israel's future was the *date* when the Messiah would appear!

Rather than go through the entire passage verse by verse, we only really need to take a look at one verse, verse 26, which will accurately pinpoint for us when the Messiah had to come.

"But after 62 weeks [434 years] the Messiah will be killed but not for Himself; then the people of the prince shall come and destroy the city [Jerusalem] and the sanctuary [the temple]; and the end thereof shall be with a flood and unto the end of the war, desolations are determined."[4]

Remember that the first temple and Jerusalem had *already* been destroyed. Now the angel is telling Daniel that in Israel's distant future the restored Jerusalem and the second temple will be destroyed also!!

What a shock that must have been to Daniel! Daniel must have been horrified to think that once again this great city of David and its sanctuary would be levelled by invading armies.

As we look back in history, we find that this prophecy came true exactly as it was told to Daniel. In 66 A.D., war broke out between the Jewish people and Rome. Four years later, in 70 A.D., the Romans finally defeated the Jewish people. The Roman prince, Titus, then destroyed the city, and the temple, and scattered the Jewish people to the four winds.

BEFORE 70 A.D.!!

The key to this prophecy for us is the information given about the Messiah.

The angel gave Daniel a chronological order of events. He said that the Messiah would come *first, and then* the city and the sanctuary would be destroyed. In other words, the angel stated clearly that the Messiah *had* to come to His people *BEFORE* the second destruction of the temple and Jerusalem, which occurred in 70 A.D.

In addition, the prophecy states that the Messiah "... will be cut off but not for himself;" that is, His death was not for Himself but for others, more specifically, for His own people.

Who came before 70 A.D, who could have been the Messiah? Who was killed before 70 A.D., but not for Himself?

As we look back in history, this description fits only one person who came at the right time, was in the right place, who fulfilled all of the Messianic prophecies and then was killed, but not for Himself. That person could only be Yeshua of Nazareth.

13

Where Is the Peace in the World?

"If Yeshua is the Messiah, then where is the peace in the world today? Wasn't that the purpose of the Messiah, to bring peace to all nations, where the lion shall lay down by the lamb?"

Yes, that is the purpose of the Messiah. But it is not His only purpose.

Some have mistakenly thought that Yeshua could not have been the Messiah because He did not usher in an era of peace.

In actuality this is a misunderstanding of what the role of the Messiah is in God's Plan of Salvation for Israel and the world.

THE DUAL ROLE OF THE MESSIAH

The purpose of the Messiah was not *just* to bring peace into the world, as wonderful as that might be.

The role of the Messiah is in reality two-fold, as is clearly taught in the Scriptures. On the one hand, we see the Messiah suffering and dying for His people, while in other passages we see the Messiah conquering Israel's enemies and setting up His kingdom.

Oddly enough, there are *more* passages about the Messiah's suffering than about His conquering!

We have already seen in Daniel where it is written that ". . . the Messiah would be killed but not for Himself." While many of the prophets spoke about the Messiah coming and eventually dying, the greatest authority among the prophets on this particular subject was Isaiah, who wrote about the sufferings of the Messiah on numerous occasions and at great length.

"He was despised and forsaken of men, a man of sorrows and acquainted with grief; and like one from whom men hide their face. He was despised, and we did not esteem Him. Surely our griefs He himself bore, and our sorrows He carried; yet we ourselves esteemed Him stricken, smitten of God and afflicted. But he was pierced through for our transgressions . . . He was cut off out of the land of the living for the transgression of my people to whom the stroke was due."[1]

The purpose of the Messiah was always far greater than simply world conquest. His greatest function as God's Anointed One was to bear our sins upon His back, and thereby carry away their terrible penalty in the sight of God.

As wonderful as world peace is, how much greater is it to be reconciled to God? There can never be true peace in the world today until our hearts are right with God our Creator.

Yeshua did not bring peace into the world when He came because that was not His purpose.

He came *first* to suffer and die for our sins. He *will* come again one day soon in power and glory to usher in an eternal era of peace throughout the world.

WIDELY ACCEPTED IN YESHUA'S DAY

While the concept of a "Suffering Messiah" might be new to some today, in Yeshua's day this concept was widely accepted within Judaism.

A Suffering Messiah may not have been the most popular Messianic idea at that time because of the Romans, but it was certainly understood biblically by the rabbis centuries before Yeshua was born.

We know this because in the Jewish writings before the time of Yeshua, these passages I have just mentioned about the Suffering Messiah and many more were ALL recognized by the rabbis in the 1st Century A.D. as referring to the Messiah.[2]

They may not have understood how the same Messiah would

both suffer and die and then come again one day in the clouds of heaven in power and glory. Nevertheless, the Scriptural evidence in the Tenach for the suffering of the Messiah was just too great to ignore.

TWO MESSIAHS?

Not only did rabbinic Judaism believe in a suffering Messiah *before* Yeshua ever appeared, but for centuries *after* Yeshua, this concept continued to have a significant place in rabbinic, messianic theology.

After Yeshua's time, though, an interesting change took place. Whereas before Yeshua, the rabbis only talked about *one* Messiah, *after* Yeshua a "new theory" developed which stated that there were actually *TWO* Messiahs. (To this day there are still some orthodox Jews who adhere to this "Two Messiah" theory.)

Basically, this theory states that there are two different Messiahs who will fulfil the two clearly dichotomous roles of suffering/dying and conquering/bringing peace.

The Suffering Messiah is called "Messiah ben-Joseph" (Messiah—son of Joseph). The conquering Messiah is called "Messiah ben-David" (Messiah—son of David).

The Messiah ben-Joseph will regather and restore Israel, so the theory goes. Eventually though, he will be killed in a great war with a world power called Gog and Magog.

Then the Messiah ben-David will appear to finish off this great victory for Israel. He will judge the nations and set up his great kingdom of peace throughout the earth.

This theory did not appear in the Talmud until the 3rd century A.D. Up until then everyone was agreed there was only one Messiah.[3]

Obviously, this "new theory" was an attempt by the rabbis to answer the claims of the first century Messianic Jews (Jewish believers in Yeshua), who boldly declared that Yeshua was the Suffering Servant of God, and could back it up with Scriptural evidence.

Since the Scriptures could not be denied as to the fact that the Messiah had to suffer and die, the only alternative was this "Two-Messiah" theory.

TAKE YOUR CHOICE!

Obviously, the "Two-Messiah" theory is fraught with flaws.

There is simply no evidence for it anywhere in the Scriptures. Nowhere in the entire Word of God or Tenach is the Messiah ever spoken of in the plural.

The prophets spoke about *one* Messiah, *one* Anointed One, *one* Redeemer and *one* Savior of Israel.

How confusing it would be to have to look for *two* Messiahs!

The Word of God is abundantly clear that there is only one Messiah. He has a *dual role* but there is still only one Messiah.

This dual role is seen in the book of Isaiah when he writes, "To the despised One [Messiah], to the One abhorred by the nation, to the servant of rulers, kings shall see and arise, princes shall also bow down; because of the Lord who is faithful, the Holy One of Israel who has chosen You."[4]

In this messianic passage we can see that at one point the Holy One of Israel will be despised and abhorred. But then later, at some future point, kings and princes will worship this same person (notice the change in verb tenses from the past tense to the future tense).

While there is only one Messiah, the "Two Messiah" theory is interesting to know because it confirms the fact that the Scriptures are clear about the Messiah's suffering and dying for His people.

Messianic Jews (Jewish believers in Yeshua) believe in *one* Messiah coming twice, while this theory teaches two messiahs coming at the same time.

Take your choice.

14

Did the Messiah Have to Die?

The evidence in the Hebrew Scriptures is clear; the Messiah *must* die. Our next question to answer is *why* must He die?

Certainly the theory of the "Two Messiahs" does not answer our question. Why we must have two military messiahs with one of them dying and the other living does not make much sense and certainly does not tell us why the first must die.

Once again, Isaiah, the expert on the Suffering Servant of God, supplies the answer, "Surely our griefs He Himself bore, and our sorrows He carried; . . . He was pierced through for our transgressions, He was crushed for our iniquities; the chastening of our well-being fell upon Him, and by His scourging we are healed."[1]

The Messiah came to die for *us*. He came to bear our sins upon himself, to make an atonement for us before God.

MISSING THE MARK

Everyone has their ideas concerning right and wrong, and how they would define sin. Put 100 people together in a room and ask them to define sin and you'll undoubtedly get 100 different answers.

But God tells us exactly what He considers sin to be in the Bible.

The very Hebrew word used for sin most often is *"chet,"* which literally means "to miss the mark" i.e., God's mark and God's standard. Other Hebrew words for sin carry the various concepts of revolt, straying, transgression, guilt and crime.

Sin in God's sight therefore is rebellion against Him and His laws.

In addition to telling us what sin is, God also makes it abundantly clear that there is not a man or woman on the face of the earth who has not sinned. ''Indeed, there is not a righteous man on earth who continually does good and who never sins . . . the Lord has looked down from heaven upon the sons of men, to see if there are any who understand, who seek after God. They have all turned aside; together they have become corrupt;there is no one who does good, not even one.''[2]

These passages are all from the Tenach, the Jewish Scriptures. Sin is not a Gentile concept, but a *JEWISH* concept, with roots going back deep into the very Torah (Law) itself.

ETERNITY WITH OR WITHOUT GOD

According to God's word, sin has three effects on us.

First of all, our sins have separated us from God (Isaiah 59:1-2). The fact that mankind is separated from God is quite evident from our very history books.

The history of the human race is not one filled with peace, goodness, kindness and love toward our fellow man.

Rather, our history has been one of wars and bloodshed. We have not had a significant era of peace in all our recorded history. The more civilized we become, the more sophisticated our weaponry. As we read our daily newspapers and hear the evening news, our ever-worsening spiritual plight becomes all the more evident.

Secondly, in addition to being separated from God, our sins have caused us to have a heart that is far from God, a heart that naturally leads us *away* from the God of Abraham, Isaac and Jacob.

The Jewish prophet, Jeremiah, described this heart condition when he said, 'The heart is more deceitful than all else and is desperately sick; who can understand it?''[3]

King David went one step further by telling us that we all

have this spiritual problem from birth, "Behold I was shaped in iniquity and in sin did my mother conceive me."[4]

Isaiah takes the condition of our spiritual heart even one step further when he makes this shocking statement, "For all of us have become like one who is unclean, and our righteous deeds are like a filthy garment."[5] This is not to say that good works are not right to do. But, to take our good works and hope that they will wash away our sins in God's sight will not work.

Finally, the ultimate result of our sins is that we cannot come into God's holy presence, not in this life or in eternity.

We will all one day have to face our eternal destiny. We do not live 70 years here on the earth, then die and go back to the dust. We have a soul (nephesh in Hebrew) and a spirit (ruach) that lives forever. When we die we pass from this life on to eternity.

The question is whether our eternity will be *with* the Lord or *separated from Him* because of our sins.

The Jewish prophet Daniel confirmed the truth of this eternal judgment when he said that we would all be resurrected one day, ". . . these to everlasting life, but the others to disgrace and everlasting contempt."[6]

Because of our sins, we cannot spend eternity with the Lord, for God's holiness cannot tolerate the presence of sin.

Sin *has* to be punished by God, for these are transgressions and crimes against Him. One day we will all stand before our Maker and have to give an account of our lives to Him.

Truly, if God left us alone with our sins we would have no hope. But God has provided a way for us to be reconciled back to Him, a way to have our sins covered, to bring us back into His presence for all eternity. That way is called "Atonement."

ATONEMENT

Atonement means "reconciliation . . . reparation for an offense or injury."

The Hebrew word that is used is "kaphar" which means "to cover, expiate, condone or cancel." "Kaphar" is basically the same word used in "Yom Kippur" or the Day of Atonement.

Once again, atonement is a Jewish concept found in the Torah.

Atonement means that while we *should* have to suffer the consequences of our sins ourselves, instead God has provided a means through which something or someone else may pay the price for our wrongdoings.

For instance, if a friend of mine commits a crime and if I am allowed to stand in his place and "pay the price" for his wrongdoing, then I have atoned for his sin.

ARE WE TOO CIVILIZED?

There is only one way that God provides for atonement in His Word and that is through the shedding of blood.

To us in our civilized, 20th century society, this method surely seems to be backward, bloody and totally inappropriate. But God gave this method for the very purpose of showing the awfulness of sin in His sight.

Before the Law was given we find Abel, Adam, Noah and Abraham, sacrificing animals to God.

When God gave the Law at Mt. Sinai to Moses we find God formalizing the practice of sacrifices when He said, "For the *life of the flesh is in the blood*, and I have given it to you on the altar to make atonement for your souls; *for it is the blood by reason of the life that makes atonement.*'"

The only place that these sacrifices could be performed was on the altar in the Temple.

The entire law was actually centered around this system of sacrifices.

Every time a Jewish person committed a sin, he was to go to the Temple and offer the appropriate sacrifice for his sin. God wanted Israel to see that every time they sinned something had to die for it.

Even the holidays and feast days were centered around the sacrificial system. For anyone familiar with the story of Passover, it was the *blood* over the doorpost of the house that kept the Angel of Death from taking the first-born child of Israel.

There were sacrifices every Shabbat (Sabbath) and there were even daily sacrifices offered every morning and evening.

Obviously, God wanted Israel to focus their entire lives around this system of shedding blood whenever they came before Him. This was meant to indelibly imprint upon their minds the awfulness of sin.

A TEMPORARY SOLUTION

The shedding of blood is God's *only* method of atoning for sin in His Word.

He allowed the blood of bulls and goats to be a "covering" for sin. He allowed them to take away the penalty of our sins as a nation for a time.

But it also became clear that simply shedding the blood of bulls and goats was not going to be enough.

This was at best a temporary solution to man's spiritual problems.

As we study the passages about the Suffering Messiah, we realize that all of these animal sacrifices were in reality looking forward to the one true and permanent sacrifice that would take away the sins of Israel and the world once and for all.

15

Yom Kippur, the Azazel and Yeshua

While the system of sacrifices taught how truly terrible sin is in the sight of God, it was also obvious that animal sacrifices were inadequate for dealing with our sins in any kind of permanent way.

This was not the fault of the Torah or the Law of Moses. The responsibility for keeping the "Mitzvot" (Commandments) was on us. The problem was that we could not obey them and kept transgressing God's law over and over again.

Everytime we sinned we needed to get another animal sacrifice for a "covering." And if the sin was willful and not in ignorance, there was no sacrifice available at all!

Obviously, something greater was needed. Something more *permanent* had to be done about our spiritual condition.

A SPIRITUAL HEART TRANSPLANT

The reason why Israel kept breaking God's commandment was because of the sinful heart which each one of us has. Just as Israel broke the Law, so every other nation would have done the same, because the sinful nature within the Jew is exactly the same as the sinful nature within the Gentile. We have *ALL* sinned before God.

Something had to be done to permanently atone for our sins, and to give us a new spiritual heart that was not sinful, but attuned to God.

God could have rejected Israel as a people and all of mankind

67

for its sins. Instead, God went one step further in His great Plan of Atonement for Israel and the world. . . . He made a New Covenant or agreement that had a far different basis to it than the Law.

"Behold, days are coming", declares the Lord, "when I will make a *new covenant* with the house of Israel and with the house of Judah, *not like the covenant* which I made with their fathers in the day I took them by the hand to bring them out of the land of Egypt, *My covenant which they broke*, although I was a husband to them," declares the Lord. "But this is the covenant . . . After those days *I will put My law within them, and on their heart I will write it;* and I will be their God, and they shall be My people . . . for I will forgive their iniquity, and their sin I will remember no more."[1]

The answer to man's problem of sin, God said, was for Him to supernaturally write His law within us. Not the 613 mitzvot or the commandments that comprise the Torah, but God's will, His standards, His mind and His heart. A New Covenant in which God will give us a "spiritual heart transplant" that will enable us to serve Him and live for Him day by day.

How would this happen?

By providing us with a perfect, permanent atonement for our sins that would permanently bridge the gap between us and God. That perfect atonement would be the Suffering Servant of God, the Messiah.

Just as the Old Covenant or Law was centered around the need for atonement through the shedding of blood, so the New Covenant would be centered around the atonement through the shed blood of the Messiah Yeshua.

The shedding of the Messiah's blood was not a temporary atonement that would *cover* our sins but an atonement that would *remove* our sins and their penalty for eternity.

When one accepts this perfect atonement, the Messiah Yeshua, the Brit Hadasha (New Covenant) says, "Therefore, if any man is in Messiah, he is a new creature; the old things passed away; behold, new things have come."[2]

THE REAL YOM KIPPUR

What the Messiah Yeshua did for us can be best understood through the biblical Day of Atonement or Yom Kippur.

Notice that I said *biblical* Day of Atonement. What is commonly practiced and taught today in Judaism is that through fasting and prayer we will receive atonement for our sins.

That is not what the Torah says though!

According to the Law of Moses, it was not fasting and prayer that brought us our atonement, but the shedding of blood on the altar in the temple.

The sacrifices on Yom Kippur were all done by the High Priest, who first made an atonement for himself and his household by the slaying of a bull.

Then he proceeded to take two male goats. The first goat was to be an offering for the sins of the nation. The High Priest performed the sacrifice while the people waited outside to see if God accepted the offering for sin.

Then the High Priest took the second goat, which was called the "Azazel" or "scapegoat." He would then ". . . lay both of his hands on the head of the live goat and confess over it all the iniquities of the sons of Israel, and all their transgressions in regard to all their sins; and he shall lay them on the head of the goat and send it away into the wilderness by the hand of a man who stands in readiness. *And the goat shall bear on itself all their iniquities to a solitary land;* and he shall release the goat in the wilderness."[3]

The purpose of this second goat was not to die but to live and to carry away the sins of the people for that year.

OUR MESSIANIC SCAPEGOAT

That is exactly what the Messiah Yeshua did!

Just as that Azazel or scapegoat carried away the sins of our people for one year, so God laid the burden of our sins upon the Messiah Yeshua for eternity.

As Isaiah said, "All of us like sheep have gone astray, each of us has turned to his own way; but the Lord has caused the iniquity of us all to fall on Him.''[4]

If God could allow a simple goat to take upon itself all of our sins as a nation for one year, *how much more* could God lay His hands, so to speak, on the head of the Messiah Yeshua and allow Him to bear all of the sins of the world for eternity?

That is the great and wonderful role of the Suffering Messiah of Israel. That is what the Messiah Yeshua did for us 2000 years ago. He is our Azazel, our scapegoat, who bore our sins off to a desolate region and allowed us to come into the New Covenant of God!

MEDIATORS

Oftentimes the question is raised, ''Why do I need a mediator or go-between? Why can't I just go to God directly and not through Yeshua?''

Once again it is the matter of sin.

We cannot come into the presence of God on our own because of our sins. We cannot hold up our good works before God and expect Him to wipe out all of our sins because of them. It probably would not balance out anyway!

God is the one who has supplied a way for us to come to Him. We have to come on *His* terms which He has so mercifully and lovingly provided.

The pattern of having a mediator or go-between has been established as God's way throughout the Bible. We have always needed an Intercessor who will bridge the gap of sin between us and God.

Moses was the mediator between God and Israel on Mt. Sinai. He was the one who received the Law from God and gave it to his people.

It was Moses who interceded on Mt. Sinai, that God might not destroy Israel because of her great sin. It was because of Moses that God turned away His wrath.

Also, in the days of the temple, it was the priests who performed all of the sacrifices for the people. The average person was not even allowed in the temple. Once again, these priests were mediators.

Even on Yom Kippur, we had our mediator, the High Priest. Only he could go into the Holy of Holies where the very presence of God was. He was the one to bridge the gap between God and Israel.

Interestingly enough, even within rabbinic Judaism today, the great need for this Messianic Atonement and for a Mediator is recognized.

In a fascinating paragraph from a Jewish prayerbook for the Day of Atonement we find this startling recognition of the atonement that must come through the Messiah:

> Though He should be exceedingly angry with His people, yet will the Holy One not awaken all of His wrath. We have hitherto been cut off through our evil deeds, yet Thou, O our Rock, hast not brought consummation on us. Our righteous anointed (the Messiah) is departed from us. He has born the yoke of our iniquities and our transgressions. He beareth our sins on His shoulder that He may find pardon for our iniquities. We shall be healed by His wound, at the time the Eternal will create Him (the Messiah) as a new creature. O bring Him up from the circle of the earth. Raise Him up from Seir to assemble us the Second time on Mount Lebanon by the hand of Yinnon.[5]

16

Who Really Killed Yeshua?

Since we are talking about the death of the Messiah Yeshua, an important issue arises, particularly in regards to the nation of Israel.

That issue is "Who killed Yeshua and who is held responsible for His death?"

The reason that this question is so important is because Jewish people have been accused for centuries by anti-Semites of being "Christ-killers" and of having the blood of Yeshua on their hands.

Obviously these people are ignorant of both history and the Word of God. It is high time to set the record straight concerning Yeshua's death.

CRUCIFIXION—A ROMAN METHOD

To find out who actually killed Yeshua, all we have to do is to go back to the very words of Yeshua Himself when He predicted to His disciples, "Behold, we are going up to Jerusalem; and the Son of Man will be delivered to the Chief Priests and Scribes, and they will condemn Him to death, and will deliver Him to the Gentiles to mock and scourge and crucify Him, and on the third day He will be raised up."[1]

Who did Yeshua say would kill Him?

The Gentiles and more specifically, the Romans, whose army and empire represented most of the nations of the world at that time.

History bears out that Yeshua's words came true.

He died through crucifixion, which was a Roman method of execution, not a Jewish one. The Jewish method would have been stoning to death.

At this particular juncture in history, Israel did not even have the authority to execute capital punishment. They were under the Roman governors, who were the only ones able to execute anyone in Israel.

So it was actually the Romans who killed Yeshua. It was Pontius Pilate who gave the final order for Yeshua to be killed, although he knew Him to be innocent. And when the Romans killed Yeshua they did so with obvious relish. They mocked Him, beat Him, gave Him a crown of thorns, vinegar to drink and after His death even divided up His clothes by lot.

THE RELIGIOUS ESTABLISHMENT

At the same time, Yeshua did say that He would be condemned by the Chief Priests and Scribes. Notice that Yeshua did not say that He would be condemned by the *people*, the masses or general populace of Israel.

There is a reason for that.

Yeshua was tremendously popular among the people. Most considered Him to be at least a great teacher and rabbi. Others considered Him to be a prophet sent by God. Many felt that He was the long-awaited Messiah.

When Yeshua made His final appearance in Jerusalem, the streets were lined with multitudes of people proclaiming Him to be the Messiah of Israel.

"And the multitudes going before Him, and those who followed after were crying out, saying, 'Hosanna [save now or salvation] to the son of David; Blessed is He who comes in the Name of the Lord; Hosanna in the highest!!!' ''[2]

These multitudes were declaring Yeshua to be the Messiah! Obviously, they did not want Him killed; on the contrary, they wanted Him on the throne! The masses were not involved whatsoever in Yeshua's death.

Yeshua said that it would be the Chief Priests and Scribes who would condemn Him. These people comprised the religious and political establishment of that day, and represented only a small fraction of the nation of Israel. Much of this religious hierarchy was corrupt and in league with Rome. As a result, many of them were actually hated by the people.

A segment of the religious establishment considered Yeshua a threat and wanted Him killed. Not all of the religious leaders, mind you. Some, even in the Sanhedrin (the highest Jewish court of law at that time), were in favor of Yeshua (Nicodemus and Joseph of Arimathea, for example). In fact, quite a number from this religious establishment eventually accepted Yeshua as their Messiah.[3]

But a few were fanatically opposed to Yeshua and plotted to have Him killed.

It was this group which came with a carefully handpicked mob late at night (for fear of the people) to capture Yeshua. It was they who condemned Him in the Jewish court and brought Him before Pontius Pilate. It was this same small minority of leaders who persuaded the mob to have Yeshua killed when Pilate offered to release either Barabbas or Yeshua.

Truly, Yeshua's words were fulfilled, as history bears out that a segment of the religious establishment plotted carefully to condemn Him, while it was the Romans who actually killed Him.

THE REAL CULPRIT

Therefore, if we view Yeshua's death strictly on a historical basis, we have to conclude that He died at the hands of the Roman army, while only a tiny portion of the Jewish nation was even involved.

Now that we have set the historical record straight, we have to come to the conclusion that NOBODY is really to blame today for the death of Yeshua.

Why? Because, first of all, nobody is to blame for what their ancestors did 2000 years ago!

Can you imagine if you found out that your great-great-grandfather had killed someone and that now someone was trying to hold you responsible for that death over 100 years later?!!?

The Jewish people are no more responsible today for what a handful of misdirected leaders did in Israel nearly twenty centuries ago, than the Gentiles are for the terrible way the Romans tortured and killed the Messiah Yeshua.

If you want to blame somebody, the only one to really blame is God!

I say this because, this was the purpose of the Suffering Messiah. He was ordained by God to come and die for the sins of Israel and world.

The Jewish prophet Isaiah tells us that ". . . the Lord was pleased to crush Him, putting Him to grief [the Messiah]." God *wanted* to do it because Yeshua was making His soul an offering for the sins of many!

God is the only one who could kill His Messiah! This was His plan from the very beginning. It was His will that Yeshua be an offering for sin for all eternity.

The only one to blame then is God! He is the only one that could have possibly killed the Messiah, and He is the one who claims to have done it!

Not the Gentiles. Not the Romans. Not the Chief Priests and Scribes. And certainly not the nation of Israel.

HE'S ALIVE!

There is one more reason why no one is to blame for Yeshua's death and that is because He's alive today.

You might have been wondering to yourself all along, how the Messiah could die, and then somehow come back again to conquer and set up His kingdom of peace.

There is only one way. The Messiah would have to be raised from the dead, ascend back into heaven and await the proper time when He could come again to usher in the Messianic era.

The Messiah's resurrection from the dead is seen when King

David prayed to God, "You will not leave my soul in Sheol neither will You allow your Holy One [the Messiah] to see corruption." Isaiah said that after the Messiah died the Lord would "prolong his days;" in other words, God would raise Him from the dead.[4]

No one is to blame for the Messiah's death because He lives today and is coming back again in power and glory! All this was part of God's marvelous Plan of Atonement for the world.

17

The Rise of Messianic Judaism

Today, there are tens of thousands of Messianic Jews (Jewish believers in Yeshua the Messiah) in the world. Estimates have run as high as 100,000 in the United States alone.

The Messianic Movement is in many ways a 20th-century counterpart to the great Messianic Movement among the Jewish people in the first century.

There have always been Jewish people who have believed in Yeshua as the Messiah. Particularly since the early 1800's, the numbers of such Jewish believers have increased dramatically.

But it was only after 1967, when Jerusalem was back in Jewish hands, that the modern movement of Messianic Judaism really came into being.

Along with the rebirth of Messianic Judaism, Messianic synagogues have sprung up throughout the United States. These Messianic congregations have proved to be the very heart and core of the movement.

Today's Messianic Jews believe in Yeshua yet continue to live as Jews.

They celebrate Jewish holidays, raise their children in Messianic day schools, fervently support the state of Israel and even live in Messianic communities within the Jewish community.

But, most important, these Jewish people have accepted Yeshua as their Messiah and believe that they have found true, biblical Judaism.

A CONTRADICTION IN TERMS?

To some people, such a movement seems to be a contradiction in terms that raises a host of questions, the biggest of which is, "Can a Jewish person believe in Jesus and still remain a Jew?"

The reason for this question is because many people have a dichotomy in their minds. On the one hand, they think you have Jews and Judaism and on the other hand, Christians and Christianity. You are either one or the other.

The moment a Jew accepts Yeshua, so this thinking goes, he "converts" over to the "other side" and is now no more Jewish, but "Christian."

Therefore the term "Christian" has become synonymous with non-Jewish or Gentile. When a Jew accepts Yeshua, he accepts the Gentile God, the Gentile religion, and has for all intents and purposes become a Gentile. He has now turned his back on his Jewish people and heritage, or so this thinking goes.

People believe this way today, only because this is how they have been taught and trained, *without actually studying the facts for themselves.*

FIRST-CENTURY MESSIANIC JUDAISM

Historically, this faith in Yeshua the Messiah is inherently Jewish.

Yeshua was a Jew. He ministered in a Jewish land among Jewish people. His disciples were all Jewish and all of his initial followers were Jewish. The writers of the New Covenant were also Jewish.

At first, this movement was considered by the Roman Empire to be just another Jewish sect because it was comprised only of Jewish people.

Nor was Messianic Judaism (as we would call it today) a small, insignificant movement, either.

Jewish people were accepting Yeshua as their Messiah in tremendous numbers. According to the Book of Acts, on two different occasions alone, there were huge crowds of 3000 and 5000 Jewish people who accepted Yeshua![1]

Since these figures only mentioned the men, the total number of Messianic Jews from these two figures alone rises into the tens of thousands when we include women and children.

These early Messianic Jews resided in Jerusalem. More than likely, they formed this huge body of believers into smaller, ''house'' synagogues.

These innumerable Messianic congregations throughout Jerusalem were all under the authority of the Jewish apostles in much the same way that the Sanhedrin was the ruling religious body for rabbinic Judaism.

Eventually, the Messianic Movement in Yeshua spilled out into the countryside of Judea and Samaria, where more Messianic congregations and synagogues were formed.

Within just a few short years, Messianic Judaism had become a prominent faith in Israel alongside the many other Jewish religious groups.

250,000 TO 1 MILLION MESSIANIC JEWS!

Nor did the first century movement of Messianic Judaism stop in Jerusalem, Judea and Samaria.

From the evidence in the New Covenant (the Book of Acts, James, 1 Peter, Hebrews), Messianic synagogues sprang up throughout the Roman empire and beyond. Wherever there were communities of Jewish people in the Diaspora, Messianic congregations were formed.

While the Messianic Movement did not encompass the entire nation or even necessarily a majority, it certainly became a highly significant segment of the population and a powerful force within the nation of Israel.

Some have estimated that in the first century alone that there were as many as 250,000 to 1 million Messianic Jews!!

They came from every walk of life, from the common people to the nobility. There were many priests and Pharisees who eventually accepted Yeshua, and even members of the ruling Sanhedrin in Jerusalem.

IS IT GENTILE TO BELIEVE IN YESHUA?

Strangely enough, the issue in the first century was not if it was Jewish to believe in Yeshua, but whether Gentiles were allowed to come into this faith in the Jewish Messiah!!

The reason for this problem was because the Torah or Law had expressly taught that Israel was a nation set apart by God to worship the one true God of Abraham, Isaac and Jacob.

They were not to fraternize with the nations. They were not to worship the idols of the surrounding peoples. They were to totally reject all paganism and be separated spiritually from the world.

While there were Gentile converts to Judaism throughout the Roman Empire, the concept of bringing Gentiles into this faith in Yeshua was still new to the early Messianic Jews.

Isaiah had predicted centuries before that the Messiah would come not only for Israel but would also be a "light to the nations."[2] In other words, the atoning work of the Messiah was for the entire world!

But this concept was still new to the early Messianic Jews. Some felt that the Gentiles would first have to convert to Judaism, be circumcised, and keep the Law of Moses.

In other words, some Messianic Jews felt that the Gentiles had to become Jews first!!!

Other Messianic Jews at that time felt that the Gentiles could come into the faith as Gentiles without having to convert.

This became such a burning issue, that in 49 A.D. the leaders in Messianic Judaism met together in a great council in Jerusalem to settle the matter.

Under the leadership of Shimon (Peter), Yacov (James) and Rabbi Saul (Paul), the assembly came to the conclusion that Yeshua was truly the Jewish Messiah *for the world* and that all nations did not have to convert to Judaism and keep all of the Law of Moses.[3]

COMPLETED JEWS

What a turnabout that is for us today!

Today people wonder if a Jewish person can accept Yeshua and still remain a Jew!

The issue with the Messianic Jews in the first century was *never* if they were still Jewish or not. Of course they were! What else could a faith in the Jewish Messiah be?!?

Not for one moment did they feel like they were "converting" to another religion. Not for one moment did they feel they had turned their backs on their Jewish people and quit being Jews.

On the contrary, they continued to live as Jews, worship as Jews, and even fight for their people against Rome. They continued daily in the temple and were greatly accepted by their own people.

They did not feel less Jewish by following Yeshua, but even more Jewish.

They viewed their acceptance of Yeshua as a *completion* of their Judaism. They were completed and fulfilled as Jews because they had found the Messiah, and had found the Atonement which God had provided for them through this Jewish Messiah.

Just as the early Messianic Jews considered themselves completed Jews, so their 20th century counterparts feel the same way today.

It truly is Jewish to believe in Yeshua the Messiah!!!

18

The Real Issue

We can talk culture, theology and history all we want and it will not necessarily answer our questions about whether or not it is Jewish to believe in Yeshua.

The real issue is not one of culture, history or theology. The real issue is not even whether or not it is *Jewish* to believe in Yeshua. The real issue is whether or not Yeshua is truly the Messiah of Israel.

If Yeshua *is* the Messiah, and if He fulfilled the prophecies concerning the Messiah found in the Tenach, then obviously it is the most Jewish thing in the world to believe in Him!

In fact, if Yeshua truly is the Jewish Messiah, then all Jewish people everywhere should accept Him without delay!

There is only one way to find out.

We all have to go back to the Word of God ourselves, study the Messianic prophecies and find out the truth about this man of Galilee. As we do this, we need to pray that God will give us understanding and an open heart. "And you will seek Me and find Me, when you search for Me with all your heart."[1]

DEMENTED, A LIAR OR THE MESSIAH?

One last thought on Yeshua.

Sometimes when a person reads about the life of Yeshua, they are impressed, at least to a certain extent. They might come to the conclusion that He was a "good man," a "good teacher," or possibly even that He was a prophet from God.

While that kind of conclusion is nice and somewhat diplomatic, it is also impossible.

For Yeshua claimed to be far more than just a righteous man, a good teacher or even a prophet like Moses. Yeshua claimed to be the Messiah. He claimed to be the Son of the living God. He said to all of us, "I am the Way, the Truth and the Life; no one comes to the Father but through Me."[2]

No prophet or rabbi ever made such a claim. And if they did, they would have to back it up with proof!

Yeshua's own words challenge us to make a decision about Him. He challenges us to set aside the assertion that He was just another good man and teacher. His own words reject that conclusion.

Since He said He was more than that, we therefore have to conclude one of three things about Him:

1) that He was *deluded or demented* for believing that He was Israel's Messiah,

2) that He was a *liar* out to deceive His people into accepting Him as the Messiah,

3) that He was *exactly who He claimed to be,* the Messiah and Savior of Israel, whom we should all accept.

The Messiahship of Yeshua is important to know. It deals with the future of Israel, the world, and our eternal destiny as well.

There is still only one way to find out. Investigate the Scriptures, go to prayer and ask the Lord to give you wisdom.

If Yeshua is the Messiah then you will find these words of His coming true in your own life:

"I am the resurrection and the life; he who believes in Me shall live even if he dies, and everyone who lives and believes in Me shall never die. Do you believe this?"[3]

SOME KEY
MESSIANIC PROPHECIES

PROPHECY	TENACH (Old Covenant)	NEW COVENANT
1. Birth of the Messiah	Isaiah 9:5–6*	Matthew 1 & 2
2. Born of a Virgin	Isaiah 7:14	Matthew 1:18–25
3. Place of Birth—Bethlehem	Micah 5:1*	Matthew 2:1–6
4. Time of the Messiah's Coming	Daniel 9:26	
5. To be a Prophet like Moses	Deuteronomy 18:15–18	Luke 7:16–17
6. To Preach, Heal and Save	Isaiah 61:1–2	Matthew 8:17
7. Enter Jerusalem on a Donkey	Zechariah 9:9	Matthew 21:1–11
8. Usher in a New Covenant for Israel	Jeremiah 31:30–33*	Matthew 26:26–28
9. The Suffering Messiah	Isaiah 52:13—53:12	
10. Rejected by His People	Isaiah 53:3	Matthew 26:3–4
11. Tried and Condemned	Isaiah 53:8	Matthew 27:1–2
12. Silent Before Accusers	Isaiah 53:7	Matthew 27:11–14
13. Mocked and Taunted	Psalm 22:7–8	Matthew 27:27–31
14. Lots Cast for His Garments	Psalm 22:18	Matthew 27:35
15. To Die with Sinners	Isaiah 53:12	Matthew 27:38–44
16. Death of the Messiah	Isaiah 53, Psalm 22, Daniel 9:26, Zechariah 12:10, 13:7	Matthew 27:45–53

17. Death By Crucifixion	Psalm 22:14–17	Matthew 27:38
18. Resurrection of the Messiah	Isaiah 53:10,	
	Psalm 16:10	Matthew 28:1–10
19. Seated at Right Hand of God	Psalm 110:1	Acts 1:1–10,
		2:33–36
20. Will Return in Clouds of Heaven . . .	Daniel 7:13	
21. . . . To the Mount of Olives	Zechariah 14:1–4	
22. To Rule in Peace & Justice	Isaiah 11	
23. Divine Nature of Messiah	Micah 5:1, Isaiah 9:5–6, 7:14, etc.	
24. Son of God	Psalm 2, Proverbs 30:4, Isaiah 48:16	
25. Sinful Nature of Man	Psalm 51:5, 14:1–3, Ecclesiastes 7:20	

*Verse number may vary with different translations.

MESSIANIC TITLES
to look for . . .

1. Messiah or Anointed One — Daniel 9:26, Psalm 2:2
2. King of Israel — Zechariah 9:9, Jeremiah 23:5-6
3. Shiloh — Genesis 49:10
4. Root or Stem of Jesse — Isaiah 11:1
5. Scepter of Israel — Numbers 24:17, Genesis 49:10
6. Star of Jacob — Numbers 24:17
7. Prophet like Moses — Deuteronomy 18:15-18
8. Holy One of Israel — Isaiah 49:7, Psalm 16:10
9. Shepherd of Israel — Ezekiel 34:20-24, Zechariah 13.7
10. Son of God — Proverbs 30:4, Psalm 2:7, 12
11. Son of Man — Daniel 7:13
12. Immanuel or "God is with us" — Isaiah 7:14
13. A Righteous Branch — Jeremiah 23, 5-6, Zechariah 6:12-13
14. Suffering Servant — Isaiah 53
15. The Lord Our Righteousness — Jeremiah 23:5, 33:16
16. Wonderful — Isaiah 9:5
17. Counsellor — Isaiah 9:5
18. The Mighty God — Isaiah 9:5
19. The Everlasting Father — Isaiah 9:5
20. The Prince of Peace — Isaiah 9:5

21. Stone, Precious
    Cornerstone   Psalm 118:22, Isaiah 28:16
22. My Fellow or My Associate   Zechariah 13:7
*23. Lamb of God   John 1:29, throughout
                                       Revelation
*24. Lion of Judah   Revelation 5:5
*25. Root and Offspring   Revelation 5:5, 22:16
    of David
*26. Bright and Morning Star   Revelation 22:16

*New Covenant Title

FOOTNOTES

CHAPTER TWO

1. Fred John Meldau, MESSIAH IN BOTH TESTAMENTS, 5th ed. (Denver, 1956), p. 3; see footnote at bottom of page, quote by Canon Dyson Hague—amended.
2. Ibid, p. 4.

CHAPTER THREE

1. Abram Leon Sachar, A HISTORY OF THE JEWS, 5th ed. (New York, 1973), p. 140.

CHAPTER FOUR

1. John D. Davis, DAVIS DICTIONARY OF THE BIBLE, 4th ed. (Old Tappan, New Jersey), pp. 49–50. "A Semitic language spoken in Aram. It was written with the same alphabet as the Hebrew, and differs from this language chiefly in the system of vocalization and in the structure of a few grammatical forms . . . it became the international language of business and diplomacy . . . it was adopted by the Jews who returned from Babylonia, and in the time of (Yeshua) was spoken by large numbers of the Jews colloquially and also by neighboring nations." Portions of the Bible are written in Aramaic i.e. Daniel 2:4–7:28, Ezra 4:8–6:18, 7:12–26. At the time of Yeshua, Aramaic had replaced Hebrew as the colloquial language in Israel.
2. Arthur E. Glass, YESHUA IN THE TENACH, pp. 1–2.
3. Matthew 1:21.

4. A.T. Robertson, WORD PICTURES IN THE NEW TESTAMENT, (Nashville, 1930), p. 10.

5. Isaiah 62:11

6. David L. Cooper, MESSIAH: HIS FINAL CALL TO ISRAEL, (Los Angeles, 1962), p. 60.

7. Habakkuk 3:13—translation from Glass, op. cit., pg. 4.

CHAPTER FIVE

1. Tim Dowley, EERDMAN'S HANDBOOK TO THE HISTORY OF CHRISTIANITY, (Grand Rapids, 1977), p. 89.

2. David Estrada and William White, Jr., THE FIRST NEW TESTAMENT, (Nashville and New York,1978), p. 133.

3. Dowley, op. cit., p. 93 (quote by F.F. Bruce).

4. James Orr, THE INTERNATIONAL STANDARD BIBLE ENCYCLOPEDIA, 2nd ed. (Grand Rapids, 1956), III, 1626.

5. Ibid.

6. JOSEPHUS: ANTIQUITIES OF THE JEWS, XVIII, iii, 3.

CHAPTER SIX

1. John 4:9

2. Alfred Edersheim, THE LIFE AND TIMES OF JESUS THE MESSIAH, (Grand Rapids, 1972), Part 1, p. 624.

3. THE INTERNATIONAL STANDARD BIBLE ENCYCLOPEDIA, II, 879.

4. Mark 6:3.

5. Matthew 21:12–13, John 2:13–17, Mark 11:16.

6. Matthew 23.

CHAPTER SEVEN

1. Isaiah 9:1–7.

2. Charles F. Pfeiffer and Howard Vos, WYCLIFFE HISTORICAL GEOGRAPHY OF BIBLE LANDS, 5th ed., (Chicago, 1978), p. 126.

3. Edersheim, op. cit., p. 224.

4. Davis, p. 256.
5. INTERNATIONAL STANDARD BIBLE EN-
CYCLOPEDIA, II, 1165.
6. Merrill F. Unger, UNGER'S BIBLE DICTIONARY, 24th
ed. (Chicago, 1976), p. 387.
7. Edersheim, op. cit., p. 225.

CHAPTER EIGHT

1. Luke 2:21.
2. Luke 2:22–24.
3. Luke 4:17, John 8:6–8.
4. Alfred Edersheim, SKETCHES OF JEWISH SOCIAL LIFE
IN THE DAYS OF CHRIST, (Grand Rapids, 1978), p. 117–118.
5. Ibid, pp. 119–120.
6. Luke 2:46–47.
7. Luke 2:49.
8. Luke 2:52.

CHAPTER NINE

1. Daniel 7:7.
2. Sachar, op. cit., p. 116.
3. Solomon Grayzel, A HISTORY OF THE JEWS, 3rd ed.
(Philadelphia, 1970), p. 89.
4. Sachar, op. cit., p. 117.
5. Isaiah 53:6.

CHAPTER TEN

1. Matthew 7:28–29.
2. Sachar, op. cit., p. 128.
3. Matthew 13:44–46.
4. Matthew 13:1–43.
5. Matthew 22:37–40.
6. Matthew 5:44–45.
7. Matthew 7:12.
8. Matthew 12:34b–35.
9. Matthew 6:19–21.

CHAPTER ELEVEN

1. Luke 7:16.
2. Jeremiah 25:11.
3. Isaiah 44:28, 48:1.
4. Daniel chapter 7.
5. Deuteronomy 18:20–22.
6. Deuteronomy 13:1–5.
7. Mark 1:7–8.
8. Deuteronomy 18:15–18.
9. Luke 21:25–28.
10. Sachar, op. cit., p. 129.
11. Matthew 23:27.
12. Ezekiel 34:1.
13. Jeremiah 23:1.
14. Isaiah 1:10.

CHAPTER TWELVE

1. John 14:6, 10:30, 14:15
2. Mark 14:62 and confirmed again by Yeshua in John 4:25–26.
3. Meldau, op. cit., p. 3—footnote.
4. Daniel 9:26—personal translation.

CHAPTER THIRTEEN

1. Isaiah 53:3–4, 8b.
2. Alfred Edersheim, THE LIFE AND TIMES OF JESUS THE MESSIAH, (Grand Rapids, 1972), see Appendix IX beginning on p. 710 and extending to p. 741, entitled, "List of Old Testament Passages Messianically Applied in Ancient Rabbinic Writings." Edersheim, a Jewish believer in Yeshua, had a special interest in this area. He compiled a list of 456 passages in the Tenach (Old Testament) that was applied to the Messiah in the most ancient Jewish writings. Included in this huge list are many "Suffering Messiah" passages that the rabbis of old also viewed as applying to the Messiah. One must conclude that the

"suffering" of the Messiah was a pillar of ancient rabbinic Messianic theology.

3. Ibid, p. 434–435.
4. Isaiah 49:7.

CHAPTER FOURTEEN

1. Isaiah 53:4–5.
2. Ecclesiastes 7:20, Psalm 14:1–3.
3. Jeremiah 17:9.
4. Psalm 51:5.
5. Isaiah 64:6.
6. Daniel 12:2.
7. Leviticus 17:11.

CHAPTER FIFTEEN

1. Jeremiah 31:31–34.
2. II Corinthians 5:17.
3. Leviticus 16:20–22.
4. Isaiah 53:6.
5. Simon Glazer, SERVICE FOR THE DAY OF ATONEMENT, Star Hebrew Publishing Co., (1928). Prayer book.

CHAPTER SIXTEEN

1. Matthew 20:17–20.
2. Matthew 21:9.
3. Acts 6:7, 15:5.
4. Psalm 16:10, Isaiah 53:10.

CHAPTER SEVENTEEN

1. Acts 2:41, 4:4.
2. Isaiah 49:6.
3. Acts 15:1–35.

CHAPTER EIGHTEEN

1. Jeremiah 29:13.
2. John 14:6.
3. John 11:25–26.